SECRETS
OF THE
VATICAN

SECRETS
OF THE
VATICAN

CYRUS SHAHRAD

GRAMERCY BOOKS

NEW YORK

Published by Gramercy Books, an imprint of Random House Value Publishing, a division of Random House, Inc., New York, by arrangement with Arcturus Publishing Limited.

Gramercy is a registered trademark and the colophon is a trademark of Random House, Inc.

Random House
New York • Toronto • London • Sydney • Auckland
www.randomhouse.com

Printed and bound in China

A catalog record for this title is available from the Library of Congress.

ISBN: 978-0-517-22994-1

10 9 8 7 6 5 4 3 2 1

Contents

Introduction

Most Sundays, the pope is little more than a white smudge – no bigger than the birds swooping from their nests in the dome of the basilica – against the high balcony of the Papal Apartments, but the mass of believers descending on the Vatican for his weekly blessing regularly fills St Peter's Square and spills into the adjoining streets.

It's a sign of the perceived purity of this most ancient of spiritual institutions – and yet controversy has dogged the Catholic Church since its days as a persecuted minority cult under the Roman Empire. The age of the Crusades, for example, or the subsequent reign of terror of the Papal Inquisition, both left the Vatican with more innocent blood on its hands than most modern dictators.

Nor are such dark days the stuff of legend alone: the 20th century also saw its fair share of Vatican cover-ups. What happened to the speech denouncing fascism that Pope Pius XI was due to give just hours before his death in 1939, and what was the true role of his successor, Pius XII, in the rise of Nazi Germany? What really happened to Pope John Paul I, found dead in 1978 after only 33 days in office? What part did the Vatican play in the events leading up to the ritualistic killing of the Italian banker Roberto Calvi in 1981? And why was the Vatican so keen to close the file on the gruesome Swiss Guard murders of 1998?

A shrewd person quickly learns to ignore any 'official' version of such events. Instead, those seeking the truth must be prepared to penetrate the Vatican's arterial corridors, peer beneath its floorboards and poke through mountains of seemingly irrelevant papers. The truth, as always, is gathering dust in the unlikeliest of places.

Those seeking the truth must be prepared to penetrate the Vatican's arterial corridors.

6

The faithful regularly flock to St Peter's Square for a glimpse of the leader of the Catholic Church.

PART ONE

The History of the Vatican

To study the development of the Church is to study the history of much of the wider world. These days, the papacy's temporal powers are largely limited, but in ancient times its flags crossed oceans and conquered entire continents, and there are few major historical events that were not affected by its grand plans.

Like all empires, however, the story of the Christian empire is one of rise and fall. It began inauspiciously in Rome, where early followers of this new, and in Roman eyes at least, bizarrely monotheistic Eastern cult were deemed heathens deserving of the most savage deaths, usually in the arena. Following the intervention of the Christian convert Emperor Constantine, Christianity experienced spectacular growth. Constantine legalized Christian worship and ordered the first St Peter's Basilica built on the site of the enormous church we see at the centre of the Vatican today.

The subsequent period of consolidation and conquest was unprecedented – with the Word of God spread by means of monasteries, missionaries and ill-advised Crusades – but the inevitable decline and fall was only centuries away. The increasing corruption and politicization of the papacy eventually came up against the shift towards humanist ideals embodied by the Renaissance; later, the secular colonization of far flung lands and revolutions in both agriculture and industry gave mankind's short term gains priority over his more long term spiritual rewards. Slowly but steadily, the power of the Holy See began to wane.

Through all this, however, one thing has remained constant within the Church, and that is the position of the pope as its spiritual leader. For this reason, the following pages provide not only a brief history of the Vatican itself, but also, on page 178, a timeline of significant events alongside profiles of the most notable popes, beginning with St Peter all the way up to the current pontiff, Benedict XVI.

What happens in the 2,000 years between them is as much a history of the world itself as it is the story of a religion.

*St Peter's
Basilica has
inspired
visitors
since its
consecration
in the year
1626.*

Eras of the Vatican

Many people argue that the modern Vatican is not an independent entity, but rather a vessel for the Catholic Church itself. So to understand how the Vatican actually works, it's best to look first at the Church itself and its evolution over the last 2,000 years – and how it has managed to shape much of the world we see today.

0-337 AD: A PALACE FOR THE PERSECUTED

Where once the pope was able to rally tens of thousands of warriors with a well-timed speech and a promise of everlasting life, these days he has to make do with a more advisory role from the spiritual sidelines. And yet, while the fortunes of the Church cannot be said to be at their best, they are at least a great deal better than during its unpromising beginnings under the Roman Empire. Back then, the only sanctified places of public worship were temples to the likes of Saturn, Mercury and Minerva, while Christianity was an illegal cult, persecuted with extreme prejudice by the authorities – and the worst was the mentally unstable Emperor Nero.

In 64 AD, Nero is reported to have sat atop the Quirinal Hill playing his lyre and singing while Rome burned for six days below him. He then blamed the fire on the Christians, whom he proceeded to

Emperor Nero's reputation for cruelty towards the cult of Christianity was legendary.

slaughter in vast numbers: some were covered in wax, impaled on poles and set on fire to illuminate Nero's garden parties ("Now you are truly the light of the world," he is reported to have joked); others were sewn up into the skins of animals and fed to the lions of the arena; many more were crucified.

One such crucifixion was that of St Peter, who had become the first Bishop of Rome – and thereby the first pope – when Jesus chose him to lead the Apostles in his absence (Peter asked to be crucified upside down, as he felt unworthy of the same death as Jesus). It may seem an inappropriate exit, but the lives of popes in those days tended to be short and their endings anything but sweet: St Clement (88-97 AD), for example, was tossed into the ocean with a ship's anchor around his neck; St Marcellinus (296-304 AD) is believed to have been thrown down a well.

Indeed, it wasn't until Constantine became Roman Emperor in 306 AD that things began to get easier for the followers of Christ. Constantine's mother Helena was a powerful Christian (she would later lead one of the first missions to the Holy Land to uncover relics including nails and chunks of the True Cross), and this clearly influenced her son. In 312 AD, while preparing for the Battle of Milvian Bridge, Constantine witnessed a vision of the cross and had Christian standards painted on his soldiers' shields. The battle was a resounding success, word spread, and attitudes towards Christians changed almost overnight. In

Constantine witnesses a vision of the cross before the Battle of Milvian Bridge.

313 AD, Constantine drafted the Edict of Milan, which allowed Christians freedom to practise their religion openly without fear of persecution, and in 326 AD, he ordered the construction of the original St Peter's Basilica on the site of the Apostle's martyrdom. By the time Constantine was baptized a Christian on his deathbed in 337 AD, this once persecuted religion was ready to begin taking over the world.

338-814 AD: FROM CONSOLIDATION TO CONQUEST

With the administrative centre of the Roman Empire relocated to Constantinople in Byzantium (now Istanbul in Turkey), there was a power vacuum that the Bishop of Rome was quick to fill, and the following 200 years was a period of significant consolidation for the Church. In 382 AD, Pope Damasus I convened the Council of Rome which may have officially codified the books of the Bible into the Old and New Testaments; monasteries were set up across Europe for the study, translation and reproduction of religious texts; and Latin, the language of educated

Pope Leo III repays the loyalty of the Frankish King Charlemagne by crowning him Holy Roman Emperor on Christmas Day 800 AD.

people across Europe, became the official language of Rome (it remains the official language of the Vatican).

But if the 200 years following the Edict of Milan was a time of papal consolidation, then the rest of the first millennium was all about expansion. By 500 AD, most of France had been converted. In 597 AD, Pope Gregory I sent St Augustine to England, where he converted the Anglo-Saxon king of Kent, Ethelbert, before setting himself up as the first Archbishop of Canterbury. In 719 AD, Pope Gregory II sent the Devon-born Wynfrith – later St Boniface – to Germany, where he founded numerous bishoprics and baptized countless locals until his death at the hands of an irate mob (he reputedly died trying to shield himself from swords with a Bible).

It would be another 80 years, however, before Christianity could become a force for conquest as well as voluntary conversion. In 799 AD, the then Pope Leo III was so unpopular (accused of perjury, adultery and selling papal pardons

known as 'indulgences') that he was dragged into the street, beaten by a crowd and threatened with having his tongue cut out.

He was then formally deposed and sent to a monastery, from where he managed to escape, eventually seeking refuge with the Frankish King Charlemagne, who accompanied him back to Rome. There, on Christmas Day 800 AD, Leo repaid Charlemagne's loyalty by crowning him head of the new Holy Roman Empire, thereby establishing the formidable Carolingian dynasty as the secular arm of the Church.

Where the Carolingians conquered, they lost no time in establishing Christianity – and few places escaped their attention. By the time he died in 814 AD, Charlemagne had helped found a Christian empire that stretched across most of Europe. From such humble beginnings, the Christian Church seemed finally on the verge of acquiring absolute power – but, as with the Roman Empire that preceded it, things were far too good to last.

815-1492: HOLY WARS, UNHOLY WORLD

The conquering spirit of the Arab world had been witnessed already when the age of holy wars began at the start of the second millennium. The prophet Mohammad had been born in Mecca in the year 570 AD, founding Islam after he began experiencing visions and writing down the revelations that would eventually form the Quran following his death in 632 AD. Six years later, a Saracen army seized Jerusalem in the name of Islam, before going on to conquer much of the Middle East, while periodically invading Europe. But it wasn't until 1009, when Islamic forces sacked the pilgrimage hospice in Jerusalem and laid siege to Constantine's Church of the Holy, that Christians became angry. In 1095, when the Byzantine Emperor Alexius I sent envoys to Rome begging for assistance against marauding Turks, that anger spilled over into rage.

Pope Urban II convened a council in France, where he made a rousing speech urging the faithful to pick up swords in the service of God, promising his holy warriors an automatic pardon for their sins and a guaranteed place in Heaven. Tens of thousands answered the call – as many zealous peasants as professionally trained knights – and the First Crusade set off, blazing a bloody trail of death and destruction all the way to Jerusalem, which was brutally recaptured in 1099.

Less than a century passed, though, before Muslim forces recaptured Jerusalem in 1187. As a result, the next two centuries saw no fewer than eight further crusades to the Holy Land, all equally bloody, but none matching the brutal success of the first.

Pope Urban II rallies the faithful to take part in the notorious First Crusade.

*Four leaders of the First Crusade:
Godefroi de Bouillon, Raimond de Toulouse,
Boemund de Tarento and Tancred d'Hauteville.*

By the 13th century, with the impotence of the Crusades becoming painfully apparent, the papacy decided to shift its religious ire on to its own people and root out heretics closer to home. In 1209, Pope Innocent III instigated the Albigensian Crusade, an attempt to crush the heretical Cathar movement in southern France; five years later, Innocent summoned the Fourth Lateran Council, which demanded Jews and Muslims wear special badges to distinguish them from Christians; and in 1232, under the instruction of Pope Gregory IX, the Inquisition was founded to target unbelievers across the Holy Roman Empire.

And yet, despite outward appearances, this was a papacy struggling to maintain a toehold in a world spiralling out of its control. The Carolingian Empire of Charlemagne had long since dissolved, and every subsequent attempt to align itself with other kingdoms had only further politicized and thus weakened the Church, resulting in its temporary relocation to Avignon, France, between 1305 and 1378. On top of that, increasing corruption within the papacy led to such deep-seated animosity among its subjects that both the Black Death (1347-51) and the eventual fall of Constantinople to the Turks (1453) were seen by many as divine retribution.

Indeed, when the murderous, lecherous and most likely incestuous Rodrigo Borgia took the papal throne as Alexander VI in 1492, not long after the Spanish Inquisition began its 354-year reign of terror, it was arguably the Church's darkest hour.

1493-1870: DECLINE AND FALL

In 1506, when Pope Julius II tore down the old St Peter's Basilica and laid the foundations of the enormous church that dominates the Vatican today, it seemed a sign that the papacy was moving with the times. In reality, however, the times were moving much too fast for the papacy to keep up with.

The Renaissance was sweeping through Europe, giving birth to a generation of artists, architects and thinkers who were looking past the 'truth-by-authority' and dogmatic assertions of the Church and into the humanist ideals of ancient civilizations to help understand and express their place in the world.

In 1510, a German priest named Martin Luther was horrified by the level of corruption he discovered on a visit to Rome. In 1517, Luther penned his indignant *Ninety-Five Theses* – a bitter indictment of the papacy's corruption – and nailed them to the door of the Castle Church in Wittenberg. In doing so, Luther unwittingly set in motion the Reformation, and paved the way for Protestantism, legalized by the Treaty of Passau in 1552, an event that effectively split the Holy See in half.

Martin Luther, a German priest, sets in motion the Reformation by nailing his Ninety-Five Theses *to the door of the Castle Church in Wittenberg.*

To make matters worse for the papacy, scientific advances were pushing the boundaries of the unthinkable, especially in Protestant countries like England, where Isaac Newton was given free rein to develop his ideas concerning gravity, relativity and spectral light – none of which sat well with the contents of the book of Genesis. The Inquisition attempted to counter dissent by stepping up its activities but it was too late: the Age of Reason (17th century) and the Age of Enlightenment (18th century)

brought to the fore such thinkers as Descartes, Voltaire, Hume and Locke, all of whom condemned the authoritarian bent of the Church.

At the same time, the Agricultural and Industrial Revolutions caused the European powers to put progress before religious obedience, again further weakening the papacy; the French Revolution, meanwhile, came close to actually ending it, with Napoleon's troops invading the Vatican at the turn of the 19th century, deposing the pope and dissolving the Holy Roman Empire more than 2,000 years after its creation. Finally,

internal revolution in the newly formed Kingdom of Italy saw the end of the Papal States in 1848 and the forced flight of Pope Pius IX in disguise.

When he returned, with an escort of French troops, Pius was quick to convene the First Vatican Council in 1869 and assert the notion of 'papal infallibility', i.e. that it is literally impossible for the pope to err in his decisions. Not that it made much difference: by the time the French troops withdrew the following year, leaving Pius a self-proclaimed 'prisoner in the Vatican', it seemed there was hardly anybody left listening to his decisions anyway.

1871-PRESENT: AN UNEASY TRUCE

The awkward status quo between the Vatican and the Italian state remained largely unchanged until 1929, when the Lateran Treaty (signed by Prime Minister Mussolini and Pietro Gasparri, Cardinal Secretary of State) secured the borders of the State of the Vatican City, establishing the world's smallest nation and giving it independent sovereignty.

This would seem to have guaranteed a security of sorts, but it has hardly spelt

out stability for the papacy, which continues to sidestep rumour and scandal on an almost daily basis. Indeed, despite what has been portrayed as a kind of papal glasnost (an opening of more doors in the Vatican Museums; the release of countless documents previously under lock and key in the Secret Archives – see page 128), there is much about the Church today that seems more secretive than ever, as the pages of this book will show.

PART TWO

Houses of the Holy

Most people approach the Vatican as tourists, guidebook in one hand, camera in the other and official audio tour secured firmly around their necks. Many are devout enough to pay their respects at the tomb of 'Good' Pope John, or to kiss the feet of St Peter, seated on his high wooden chair inside the basilica, but few would consider climbing the 28 steps of the Scala Santa on their knees, stopping on every stair to recite a prayer.

Even fewer, it seems, would consider deviating from the tried and trusted Vatican tour: a rubbernecking sprint through the basilica, an awed, if congested slog through the museums and – time permitting – a hasty cup of coffee and a ciabatta in St Peter's Square.

Those who do want to look deeper, however, will find very few of the Vatican's less salubrious secrets written into the official guidebook – which is exactly why we've included this chapter, a roundup of the most interesting and unusual nooks and crannies of the Vatican.

In the basilica, for example, we relate the strange stories behind the supposedly super-sacred relics, the 20th century discovery of St Peter's remains beneath the high altar, and the demented Australian geologist who attacked one of the most valuable works of art on earth with a hammer. In the museums, we learn about the cursed papal

apartments of the despotic Pope Alexander VI and the history of the bizarre Egyptian obelisk in the centre of St Peter's Square.

Finally, we examine the papacy's seeming obsession with the art world and reveal the scandal that surrounds some of the art in the Vatican collection – and also uncover a suspected forgery within the Holy See's collection that could well be worth even more than the original on which it is based.

Those who want to look deeper will find very few of the Vatican's shocking secrets written into the official guidebook.

Pope Benedict XVI (2005 –), and behind him the masses congregating in St Peter's Square to bask in his holy blessing.

Shock and Awe

Against the rusty brown patchwork of central Rome, cinder grey St Peter's Basilica is one of the few landmarks it's possible to pick out from the plane window. Up close, it's even more astonishing, the sheer scale of its looming façade and formidable dome leaving most tourists lost for words – which is exactly the idea.

The largest church in the world occupies the site of Constantine's original basilica, commissioned in 326 AD to mark the place of St Peter's martyrdom and completed 30 years later. By the 15th century, this first basilica, dangerously unstable and with entire walls on the verge of collapse, was in dire need of repair. Work did not properly begin until the reign of Julius II (1503-1513), who tore down almost the entire building under the watchful eye of his master architect, Donato Bramante (nicknamed 'Bramante Ruinante' by some horrified traditionalists), and then laid the foundation stone for the new church himself.

Bramante died in 1514, after which numerous architects and artists were called in to scrutinize and rework the plans, including Raphael, Peruzzi, Michelangelo (who was personally responsible for designing the mighty Florentine dome) and Carlo Maderno, who completed the imposing façade.

On 18 November 1626, more than a century after work began, Urban VIII consecrated the new St Peter's, and the faithful began flocking from across the world to marvel at its beauty. They too were most likely left speechless.

Up close, the basilica is even more astonishing, the sheer scale of its looming façade leaving most tourists lost for words.

The artist Michelangelo was largely responsible for the design of the basilica's mighty Florentine dome.

Approaching Perfection

As you approach the basilica, you can pick out certain details of the towering façade not obvious from a distance: the central balcony, for example, from which new popes are presented to the people and give their inaugural blessings, or the 13 statues that line the balustrade (Jesus, John the Baptist and 11 of the Apostles – St Peter's statue is inside).

Entrance to the basilica itself is through one of five enormous doors in the atrium (the ornamental central door – known as the Porto di Filerete – was built for the original basilica in 1445), although it's usually a slow process thanks to the hordes of tourists stopped just inside, jaws on the floor as they struggle to take in the almost other-worldly dimensions of the interior. To help put things into some kind of perspective, the authorities long ago marked up a series of boastful bronze lines on the floor, comparing the size of St Peter's (212m long) to its closest competitors the world over, with St Paul's Cathedral in London sliding into second at 158m long.

Also on the floor, a few feet inside the entrance, is a circle of dark red porphyry stone, 2m in diameter. Of six such stones that decorated the floor of Constantine's original basilica, this is the only one that remains, and it was on this very slab that kings and emperors would have knelt to receive their coronations from the pope himself – including Charlemagne, crowned the first Holy Roman Emperor on Christmas Day, 800 AD.

The Beauty and the Beast

On 21 May 1972, a deranged Australian geologist named Lazlo Toth vaulted the barriers and set about smashing the Pieta with a hammer. In this picture, shocked bystanders are seen dragging him away from the statue.

Upon entering the basilica, most tourists head straight for the world-famous Pieta of Michelangelo, on display in the Chapel of St Peter to the right of the entrance. Michelangelo was in his 70s when Pope Paul III commissioned his work on the basilica itself, but he produced this diminutive marble statue of Jesus in the arms of Mary when he was just 23 years old, signing his name along the sash of Mary's mantle to silence doubters who deemed him too young to have come up with a work of such extraordinary depth.

These days, the signature is visible only with a pair of binoculars: the Pieta was placed behind bullet-proof glass following an incident on 21 May (Pentecost Sunday) 1972, when an Australian geologist named Laszlo Toth vaulted the barriers and attacked the statue with a hammer while shouting: "I am Jesus Christ, risen from the dead." He managed to sever Mary's arm at the elbow, shatter her nose and chip one of her eyelids before being apprehended by the authorities. He was later declared insane and unfit to stand trial.

Toth was subsequently deported back to Australia and faded into obscurity, but his influence resonates to this day: 'Lazlo Toth' became a pseudonym for several books of satirical letters by the writer and comedian Don Novello.

In an ironic postscript to Toth's attack, the Vatican announced around six months afterwards that restorers had discovered a previously unknown monogram sculpted from the skin lines on the palm of the Madonna's left hand: an 'M' for Michelangelo.

How the Pieta *looked before Toth attacked it – notice how Mary's arm is still in place.*

The Pilgrim's Progress

While tourists are jostling each other for a peek at the *Pieta*, the faithful instead tend to flock further up the hall to pay their respects at one of two monuments. The first of these is the tomb of 'Good' Pope John XXIII, who had become the most beloved pontiff in modern history when he died in 1963; the second is the statue of a seated St Peter, rescued from the original basilica and widely believed to have been sculpted in the workshop of Arnolfo di Cambio.

Peter's left hand clasps the keys to the Kingdom of Heaven, while his right is raised in a papal blessing. It is his feet, however, that get the most attention, the right one having been subjected to kisses

St Peter's bronze foot has been worn almost flat by the hands and lips of penitent pilgrims: to this day, queues of the faithful snake their way through the basilica.

The ancient statue of St Peter, a stone's throw from the site of the saint's grisly martyrdom and the recent discovery of his remains.

from the pious lips of so many pilgrims over the ages that it has been visibly worn down (as shown in the picture, visitors tend simply to clasp it in one hand these days, although whether this is over a concern for the preservation of fine art or a fear of catching some orally-transmitted disease is unclear).

Remains of the Day

From the blackened skull of John the Baptist in the church of San Silvestro to the chains reputed to have shackled the Apostle Peter in Jersusalem, now kept under the main altar of San Pietro in Vincoli, relics form the nucleus of many churches across Rome – and St Peter's Basilica is no exception.

The holiest of holies at one time included the head and a little finger of St Andrew; fragments of the True Cross brought back from Jerusalem by Constantine's mother, St Helena; the veil used by St Veronica to wipe sweat from Jesus' forehead as he carried that same cross to Calvary (and later believed to have displayed miraculous properties, from curing blindness to resurrecting the dead); and the lance of the Roman soldier Longinus, used to pierce the side of the crucified Christ.

Each is represented by a monumental statue on one of the four pillars supporting the great dome (Longinus, for example, is shown miraculously recovering his sight, while St Helena carries an enormous cross), and underneath each is a small reliquary built to house the relics themselves. Not all of them remain in the Vatican today, however. In 1964, Paul VI ordered the head and finger of

An ancient reliquary housing what are believed to be fragments of the True Cross.

A depiction of the miraculous veil used by St Veronica to wipe sweat from Jesus' forehead.

St Andrew to be sent back to the Greek city of Patras, where he was crucified, while the ancient Italian Abbey of Monoppello, high in the Apennine Mountains, was in 1999 declared to have been in possession of the 'real' Veronica's Veil all along – despite the fact that the Vatican still brings out its own version once a year for ceremonial purposes.

The lance that pierced the side of the crucified Christ is one of the most holy relics in history.

Unearthing the Apostle

The site of St Peter's martyrdom had already been drawing pilgrims from across the world for nearly 2,000 years when Pope Pius XII announced, in his pre-Christmas message of 1950, that the Apostle's tomb had been discovered beneath the high altar of the basilica.

This was the result of more than a decade of intense archaeological excavations. The crypt beneath St Peter's had long been the final resting place of popes, emperors and early Christian

authority figures, but it was always suspected that under them lay even more ancient graves – and this is exactly what the excavation discovered between 1939 and 1949, under the direction of one Ludwig Kaas, administrator of the basilica and a high-ranking Vatican priest.

In fact, what they uncovered was beyond their wildest expectations: an entire network of 2nd and 3rd century mausoleums, some Christian, some Roman. Most breathtaking, however, was a small monument dating

from as early as 160 AD and seeming to mark the tomb of St Peter. The team dug deeper, coming across a range of bones that were immediately sent to Dr Riccardo Galeazzi-Lisi, the bogus personal physician to the pope himself, who asserted (with characteristic inaccuracy) that they belonged to a powerfully built man who had died in his late 60s – a claim that led directly to Pius XII's declaration. When the bones were sent to a secular specialist for a second opinion, however, the results were far from what the Church had been hoping for: the 'apostolic remains' were in fact bones belonging not to one man, but to two separate men (one young, one much older), a woman, a pig, a chicken and a horse.

The news was hugely disappointing, and the discoveries in the Vatican Necropolis, as it came to be known, were kept from the public – until Kaas died, that is, less than two years later. It was then that an epigraphist working on the project inadvertently stumbled upon a collection of bones excavated in secret from a second tomb by Kaas himself – who had taken to working out of hours, hiding his findings from what

he saw as the heavy-handed scientific approach of the archaeological team.

When these were tested and confirmed to have belonged to a man in his 60s, the new Pope Paul VI made his own announcement, this time asserting that there could be no doubt: the relics of St Peter had indeed been found beneath the high altar of the basilica. As to what else is down there, we can only speculate.

In 1950, Pope Pius XII announced that the tomb of St Peter had been discovered.

Hallowed Halls of History

The Apostolic Palace is famous for containing the Vatican Museums, but this complex also boasts the residence of the pope himself, offering visitors a rare opportunity to walk in the hallowed footsteps of many a holy father.

In peak season, queues for the Palace's museums snake the length of the northern and eastern walls of the Vatican, while browsing the galleries themselves has been memorably described as akin to 'attempting to read metaphysical poetry in a rugby scrum'.

Such popularity, however, has as much to do with the quality of the exhibits as it does with the fact that the museums offer mere mortals a unique opportunity to wander the hallowed halls of the papal apartments, which have for centuries served as the 'religious' residence of the popes (their secular office, as heads of the papal states, was in the Quirinal Palace until the revolution of 1870).

Since 1903, popes have occupied a ten-room papal apartment on the top floor of the Apostolic Palace, which tradition dictates is renovated by every incoming pontiff. The accession of Benedict XVI in 2005 saw a major three month refurbishment to update what workers described as a painfully outmoded residence (faulty wiring, rusting pipes, a leaking roof and a decrepit central heating system).

The Apostolic Palace veiled in the enormous shadow of St Peter's Basilica.

They also updated the papal library so that Benedict would have somewhere to store his vast collection of well over 20,000 books.

Walking in His Footsteps

The current papal apartments are obviously off limits to the public, but the Vatican Museums have grown haphazardly into and around the Apostolic Palace since their creation in 1503, with the pope so close by that sections of the museum are regularly shut off when he needs to use them.

Not that there is anything stopping visitors from wandering around some of the older papal apartments. Those formerly belonging to Julius II constitute one of the most popular parts of the museum, spectacularly decorated as they are by the artist Raphael.

There are also the more controversial chambers of the despotic Borgia pope, Alexander VI, the frescos of which – by the Renaissance painter Pinturicchio – use a complex system of religious iconography to emphasize the supposedly divine origins of the Borgias themselves.

So pervasive was the lingering sickness of Alexander's reign that his successor, Julius II, refused point blank to occupy the apartments of 'that wretch', while the deeply spiritual Alexander VII had one offending fresco removed.

Recently re-discovered, it shows the pope kneeling before a Madonna reputedly modelled on his married mistress Giulia

Farnese, and clasping the foot of a baby that may well have been intended to represent one of their illegitimate children.

The current papal apartments, shown here during Easter 2005, are private, but the older papal apartments can be visited by all and sundry.

Squaring Up

The relocation of the ancient obelisk now at the centre of St Peter's Square was one of the most complex and ambitious architectural feats of the 16th century.

As the main public entrance to the Vatican, St Peter's Square is where the hubbub of holy blessings meets the highest level of petty crime in the world (despite being the only place in the Vatican where sanctified Swiss Guards patrol alongside the secular Roman police force), and it's also been the site of more than its fair share of historical dramas – the attempted assassination of Pope John Paul II in 1981, for example, or the improvised exorcism that he conducted on a hysterical 19-year-old girl in 2000.

The 40m(131ft)-high obelisk at its centre dates from the 13th century BC, and was initially used to mark the middle of the Caligula Circus (later the Nero Circus) in 1st century Rome. Its second relocation, in 1586, was the most ambitious project of the architecturally daring Pope Sixtus V, who initially offered the task to Michelangelo, who turned it down on the grounds that he thought it would topple and break.

In the end, Domenico Fontana undertook the job using an elaborate

Statues of Jesus, John the Baptist and 11 of the Apostles overlook St Peter's Square, the sheer scale of which can only be appreciated from the air.

scaffold, hundreds of ropes and dozens of teams of men all heaving together simultaneously. In 1817, a series of circular stones was set into the paving of the square to mark the tip of the obelisk's shadow as it moves in and out of the various signs of the zodiac. This effectively turns the courtyard of the square into an enormous and imposing sundial.

For Art's Sake

The halls of the Vatican boast a constantly expanding showcase of art and artefacts from around the world, proving the extent of papal pulling power when it comes to collecting and commissioning treasures of all kinds.

Begun in 1503 by Pope Julius II, the Vatican Museums were opened around the same time as the second St Peter's Basilica. Then, as now, they were intended to represent the accumulated cultural wealth of popes past and present, who had unrivalled bidding power when it came to the collection of art: no artist in his right mind would be foolhardy enough to turn down a papal commission, and besides, the Vatican coffers were virtually bottomless.

As such, the museums divide into various galleries like the Museo Pio Cristiano, filled with ancient Christian antiquities (including a stone relief of the monogram of Christ witnessed by Constantine and placed on the shields of his soldiers in 312 AD), or the Museo Pio Clementino, begun in the 18th century and now housing the world's largest collection of classical Roman statues. On top of this, there are galleries covering everything from ancient

RAPHAEL PINXIT.

Egyptian and Etruscan civilizations all the way up to the present day, with a collection of more modern artists (including Picasso, Klee and Kandinsky) compiled to celebrate the ailing Pope Paul

INITIAL

IN AEDIBVS
VATICA
NIS.

Raphael's School of Athens *depicts the artist's contemporaries, including Da Vinci, as ancient philosophers.*

Rooms, commissioned by Pope Julius II, who more or less discovered the young artist and gave him a free reign over the entire wing. The result is simply breathtaking. Perhaps most famous is his *School of Athens* in the papal study, in which his contemporaries turn up as various ancient philosophers – Da Vinci as Plato, Michelangelo as Heraclitus and Bramante as Euclid – although similarly stunning are the representations of the Mass of Bolesna (which features an early Swiss

VI's anniversary, but badly received, and largely ignored ever since.

Instead, most visitors prefer to spend time in the unfeasibly ornate Raphael

Guard) and the conversion of Constantine to Christianity, in which the Roman Emperor is seen witnessing a vision of the cross in the October sun as it splits the gathering cloud.

Labour of Love

Michelangelo's iconic Creation of Adam *forms the centrepiece of the Sistine Chapel ceiling.*

If ever an example was needed to reveal just how in love the Vatican is with art, and the kind of incredible pressure it has put on its artists to create masterpieces, it's the Sistine Chapel.

Ironically, Michelangelo was new to the discipline of fresco painting when Julius II commissioned him to undertake work on the chapel ceiling, possibly at the insistence of his then master architect Bramante, who was jealous of the young artist and wanted to see him fail. Bramante even offered to fix a scaffold to the ceiling with ropes, but Michelangelo refused – he was afraid the fixings would leave holes – and instead constructed his own free-standing 18m-high structure.

It was on this that he spent the following four and a half years, in a state of constant discomfort as he worked away at a sequence of Bible stories – from

To access the Sistine Chapel ceiling, Michelangelo designed his own 18m-high scaffolding.

The Separation of Light from Darkness to *The Drunkenness of Noah* – featuring no less than 300 characters, despite the fact that he was originally commissioned to paint only the twelve Apostles. The money was good (he pocketed in less than five years what most artists of his day would have earned in 15), but by the time the work was finished, Michelangelo was a man on the verge of a nervous breakdown.

Michelangelo's bleak depiction of The Last Judgement dominates the far wall of the Sistine Chapel.

This made it all the more difficult to return to the chapel when Paul III called him back there in 1535, now aged 60, to create *The Last Judgement* on the wall behind the high altar. The bleakness of this work is seen as a reflection of Michelangelo's depressive state of mind due to recent events – most notably the rise of Protestantism and the ravages of the Reformation – and the depiction of souls alternately rising to Heaven or being damned to Hell ranges from the graphic to the downright gruesome, with Michelangelo's own grim face peering from the folds of a sheet of human skin held by St Bartholomew.

Despite this, it was the immodesty of the piece, rather than its inherent misery, that riled the censors of the time, leading to a disastrous chiselling away and repainting of various private parts with fig leaves and loincloths at the request of Pope Pius IV in 1565 (the artist chosen to undertake this thankless task, Daniele da Volterra, spent the rest of his life saddled with the less-than-affectionate nickname 'Il Braghettone' – 'the breeches maker').

Forgeries in the Vatican

Inevitably for an institution so inextricably tied up with the art world, the Vatican has throughout history found itself occasionally embroiled in issues of forgery. This usually takes the form of arguments over the authenticity of various religious relics (how many skulls could John the Baptist have possibly had?), but it also sometimes touches more traditional works of art, as the recent intrigue surrounding the infamous Laocoön statue goes to prove.

The statue, depicting a mythical figure of ancient Greece, was long assumed to be either a Greek original or a Roman copy. Recently, however, the art historian Lynn Catterson has put forward evidence to suggest that it

The Laocoön statue is a historical whodunnit without an answer but either way, the Vatican has its hands on a genuine masterpiece.

*The Laocoön statue –
a forgery by none
other than Michelangelo
himself?*

may actually be a 16th-century forgery by none other than Michelangelo himself. Her theory is based around a sketch of Michelangelo's currently residing in the Ashmolean Museum in Oxford, England, which depicts the naked back of a man almost identical to that in the sculpture. The picture is dated 1501; the Laocoön was discovered five years later.

It would certainly tie up a few loose ends. The statue was described by the ancient Greek writer Pliny the Elder as being carved from one block of marble, but the Laocoön in the Vatican is constructed from seven separate pieces. It would also explain several seemingly unused blocks of marble that Michelangelo bought around the same time, not to mention a string of mysterious deposits in his bank account. All told, it's a historical whodunit without an obvious answer, but either way, the Vatican has its hands on a genuine masterpiece.

A Perfect Picture of Scandal

Not all of the Vatican's artworks can boast a spotless reputation: indeed, scandal surrounding the commission and completion of Vatican artworks peppers its 2,000 year history. The popes themselves can take a certain amount of credit for the partial collapse of one of the most dramatic ruins in Rome, the mighty Colosseum, which was quarried for materials during the rebuilding of St Peter's, while Pope Urban VIII also allowed the artist Bernini to strip the Pantheon of its bronze beams, which were then melted down for his baldachin above the high altar of the basilica.

Scandal also played itself out between the artists themselves, so desperate were they to secure the admiration (and thus guarantee themselves the financial support) of the popes. The 16th century artist Giovanni Lanfranco, for example, almost died while painting the frescos inside the domed ceiling of the Sant'Andrea della Valle – the highest in Rome bar St Peter's – allegedly after the scaffolding on which he was working was sabotaged by his arch rival Domenico Zampieri.

Some of the work itself is also shockingly grim. Horrifying 16th-century frescos in the Santo Stefano Rotondo depict saints being tortured and torn apart, boiled alive and burned at the stake, while the 17th century crypt of the Santa Maria della Concezione is ornately decorated with the bones and skulls of over 4,000 Franciscan friars collected between the years 1528 and 1870. The reason? A reminder, according to the plaque, that 'you will be what we are now'.

Paintings for Pardons

Such is the Vatican's love and desire for art, that a single painting has been known to garner a killer a pardon from execution. After murdering his opponent in a tennis match a few years earlier, the exiled artist Caravaggio painted the gloomy *David With The Head Of Goliath* – now on display in the sprawling Galleria Borghese – and sent it to the Vatican in an attempt to secure a papal pardon and commute the death sentence hanging over him (he superimposed his own face on the decapitated Goliath's to show how sorry he was). The pardon was granted but unfortunately for Caravaggio at least, he was mistakenly arrested on the way to Rome and died in captivity.

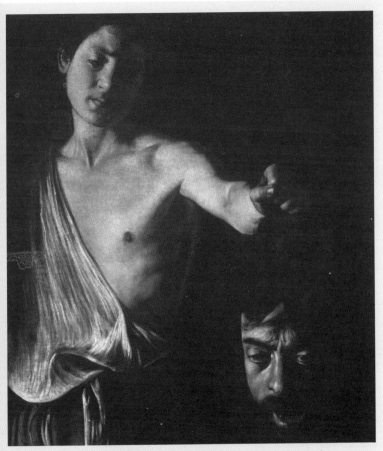

*A painting goes a long way with the papacy – this picture by Caravaggio
given to the Vatican saved him from the death sentence.*

This map of Vatican City highlights the most notable points of the papal powerbase.

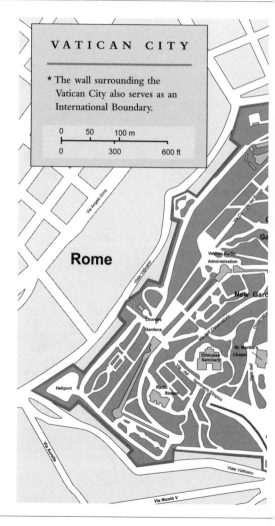

VATICAN CITY

★ The wall surrounding the Vatican City also serves as an International Boundary.

| 0 | 50 | 100 m |
| 0 | 300 | 600 ft |

Via Angelo Emo

Via Leone IV

Rome

Viale Vaticano

Vatican Radio
Administration

Ga

New Gard

Lourdes
Gardens

Viale Osservatorio

Osservatorio

St. Martha's
Chapel

Ethiopian
Seminary

Viale dell'

Heliport

Radio
Station

Via del Seminario Etiopico

Via Aurelia

Viale Vaticano

Via Nicolò V

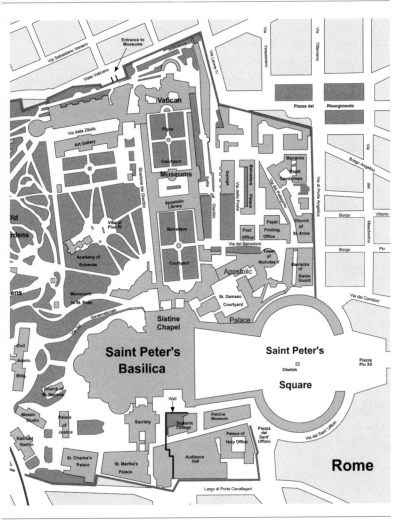

Via Sebastiano Veniero

Entrance to Museums

Viale Vaticano

Via Leone IV

Via Veigaselato

Via Ottaviano

Piazza del Risorgimento

Vatican

Via della Zitella

Pigna

Art Gallery

Courtyard

Museums

Apostolic Library

Stazione del Giardini

Salita del Giardini

Via della Posta

Garage

Belvedere Palace

Via del Pellegrino

Via di Porta Angelica

Borgo Angelico

Barracks of Papal Gendarmes

Old

Villa of Pius IV

Belvedere

Post Office

Papal Printing Office

Church of St. Anne

Borgo

Maschenno

Vittorio

Gardens

Academy of Sciences

Courtyard

Via del Belvedere

Tower of Nicholas V

Borgo

Pio

ens

Monument to St. Peter

Via del

Governatorato

Apostolic

St. Damaso Courtyard

Barracks of Swiss Guard

Via dei Corridori

Sistine Chapel

Palace

Saint Peter's Basilica

Saint Peter's

Obelisk

Piazza Pio XII

Square

Civil Admin. Bldg.

Church of St. Stephen

Mosaic Studio

Palace of Justice

Railroad Station

Wall

Sacristy

Teutonic College

Petrine Museum

Palace of Holy Office

Piazza del Sant' Uffizio

Via del Sant' Uffizio

St. Charles's Palace

St. Martha's Palace

Audience Hall

Largo di Porta Cavalleggeri

Rome

PART THREE

Life in the Vatican

In the following section we examine everyday life in this most
enigmatic and richly traditional of places, and look at how daily
existence in the shadow of St Peter's is shaped by the arcane
mechanics of the papacy.

We begin with a look at the historical role of the pope himself, and in particular how three pontiffs in the 20th century alone have attempted to mould the Catholic Church in their own images:

from the schoolmasterly Pius XII and his successor, 'Good' Pope John XXIII, to the 'Outdoor Pope' John Paul II, whose maverick spirit infuriated his aides just as often as it inspired his admirers.

We then turn to a study of the eccentricities of the Vatican's sovereignty – from its ATMs (the only ones in the world to offer a service in Latin) to the colourful Swiss Guard, the officers of which have sole responsibility for security within the Vatican's borders. This is followed by a rare insight into the ancient ceremony of conclave, convened behind the closed doors of the Sistine Chapel to elect a new pope and subject to some of the severest vows of secrecy on earth.

There's also a shocking study of the Vatican's ongoing efforts to secure its own ends by manipulating the world's media – from closing down dissident papers to burying official reports that contradict the Catholic line – while our last chapter deals with the role of women in the hugely male-orientated world of the Church, including windows into the lives of such formidable females as Countess Matilda of Tuscany, Queen Christina of Sweden and the mythical Pope Joan. A man's world the Vatican may be, but nothing is ever that cut and dried in the cradle of Christianity.

Life in the Vatican is shaped by its perceived closeness to God, with religion permeating everything from politics to the postal system.

Pope and Personality

It takes roughly ten minutes before first-time visitors to Rome are struck by the astonishing number of priests and nuns. Rosaries seem as common a sight as wristwatches; white collars as prevalent as silk ties. Religion is big business in the Vatican, and its agents are everywhere, but it's the big boss who calls the shots – and he's never far away.

If you're tall enough and timely enough, you may well catch sight of the pope himself on an ordinary trip to the city. If you do, you'll immediately realize that he's more than just the head of the Vatican: at the pontifical high mass in St Peter's Basilica, when the choir calls to him 'Tu es Petra' ('You are Peter'), it's a reminder that he is also first in a

The reaction of many upon seeing the pope is to wail, weep and fall to their knees – a sign of just how powerful the papal legacy is to devout Catholics.

direct line leading all the way back to the original Bishop of Rome, the Apostle Peter, and thereby to Jesus himself. The reaction of many (wailing, weeping, falling to their knees at his blessing) is a sign of just how powerful a link this is.

As such, a cult of personality very quickly attaches itself to the leader of the Catholic Church. Sure, popes tend to dress the same and bless the same, but on a deeper level they, like everyone else, have their own unique characteristics and idiosyncrasies. The result is that the entire Church shapes itself around the nature of its current pontiff – as a quick look at three very different popes from the 20th century reveals.

A statue of St Peter, the first pope, overlooking the site of the Apostle's martyrdom.

Pius XII to 'Good' Pope John

Few popes have been as austere or impenetrable as Pius XII (1939-1958), whose hawkish face and bespectacled, unsmiling eyes became an embodiment of the Church at its strictest and most schoolmasterly. So seriously did Pius take his role that he expected subordinates to kneel even when he was speaking to them over the phone (usually to give orders without so much as a greeting or goodbye), while groundsmen were forced to disappear from sight any time the pope chose to take a stroll in the Vatican Gardens. It was no surprise when, in 1950, Pius became the first pope to invoke 'papal infallibility' – the doctrine whereby certain papal declarations, delivered under certain conditions, are regarded as incapable of being wrong.

But if Pius was a hardline headmaster of the Holy See, then his successor,

Serious and severe, Pius XII was the most schoolmasterly of modern popes.

John XXIII (1958-1963), was its favourite uncle. The size of his paunch was matched only by his personality: affable and hugely down to earth, 'Good Pope John', as he became

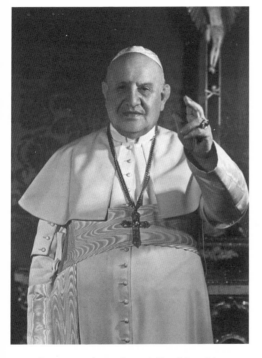

Humorous and warm hearted, 'Good' Pope John was the antithesis of his predecessor.

asking a visiting dignitary to stay for dinner – John announced within days of his election that he had scrutinized the Scriptures and found no evidence that a pope should take his meals in solitary, thereafter dining with company on almost every day of his reign. Where Pius had invoked the notion of papal infallibility as defined by the First Vatican Council in 1869, John set up the Second Vatican Council (1962-1965), which paved the way for enormous liberalizing changes and ushered in what more forward-thinking Catholics saw as a 'new springtime' in the Church. Where Pius had frowned, John smiled –

known, was always ready with an amusing joke or a terrible rambling story that had his aides tearing out their hair in frustration. Where Pius XII had always eaten alone – only once

and it made him the most beloved pope of the modern age. To this day, queues of well-wishers waiting to pay their respects at his tomb regularly snake around St Peter's.

The 'Outdoor Pope'

No pope has left his mark on the modern papacy like John Paul II (1978-2005). A Polish national, John Paul was the first non-Italian pontiff since the 16th century; he was also a former poet, playwright and actor, not to mention an avid skier and football player (a formidable goalkeeper, by all accounts).

Such a worldly background led to his impatience with much of the ceremonial stiffness of Church affairs. One of his first acts as pope was to give a highly unorthodox press conference, during which he jokingly responded to a question about whether he'd ever ski again ("I don't think they'll let me," he said, gesturing to the line of cardinals behind him).

He also referred to himself as 'I' (the more formal 'we' was henceforth banned, even from important papal documents), going so far as contacting the head of the Vatican's official newspaper and insisting that the traditional preface for directly quoting the pope – 'Following is the allocution by His Holiness as we have gathered His words from His august lips' – be replaced with a simple 'the pope said'.

It was in his popular role as the 'Outdoor Pope', however, that John Paul II most infuriated and inspired. He seemed to find the walls of the Vatican claustrophobic, regularly frustrating his minders by slipping out into the streets of Rome – sometimes in disguise – to visit friends or simply soak up the city air. Reluctant to abandon his athletic past, he also had a swimming pool built in the papal summer residence at Castel Gandolfo. Much to the Vatican's embarrassment, paparazzi snaps of him in his trunks would later appear in a notable Italian magazine.

John Paul II was the best-travelled pope in history, making 104 trips abroad.

He was also the most well-travelled pope in history, making no less than 104 pastoral trips during his pontificate, many of them to countries that had never before hosted a papal visit. Close aides began to fret, saying

that only bad things could come of such unchecked wanderlust; ironically, when the assassin's bullets finally found John Paul, it was on his own doorstep, as he entered St Peter's Square to address a gathering crowd in May 1981. The pope was lucky to survive the attempt on his life, going on to reign for more than two subsequent decades: when he did finally pass away, in 2005, it was after a 13-year struggle with Parkinson's Disease that he conducted, as with everything in his life, with characteristic warmth and public openness.

John Paul II redefined the role of the modern pope, constantly on the move and seldom out of the public spotlight. His death, in 2005, was mourned all over the world.

Pomp and Circumstance

Few things can be used to gauge papal personalities better than their attitudes towards the ancient coronation ceremony. The inauguration of Pope Pius XII, in 1939, was one of the most self-consciously elaborate in history: six hours long and involving various world leaders and dignitaries, it was also the first to be filmed and broadcast live on radio. By the late 1960s, however, the liberalizing forces of Pope John XXIII's Second Vatican Council were taking effect, and when the ill-fated Pope John Paul I was crowned on 26 August, 1978, he astonished the world by dissolving the entire ceremony and instead beginning his papacy at a solemn outdoor mass, with a simple wooden chair where the ornate papal throne would have been and a mitre instead of the traditional three-tiered tiara.

At his coronation in 1978, Pope John Paul I passed up the traditional three-tiered papal crown in favour of a pallium – a simple white woollen collar adorned with crosses – and in doing so changed the face of papal inaugurations for years to come.

John Paul II rescheduled his coronation ceremony so as not to interfere with an important football match being broadcast that evening on Italian television.

His successor, John Paul II, not only followed suit with a ceremony bereft of pomp or paraphernalia, he even asked for it to be rescheduled for the morning so as not to interfere with an important football match being broadcast that evening on Italian television. Papal authorities were understandably appalled; the Italian people couldn't have been more thankful.

Quirks of Vatican Autonomy

Not only does the Vatican lay claim to having the largest church in the world, it also boasts the dubious honour of being the smallest independent nation on earth – although its diminutive size doesn't stop it from rubbing up ordinary Romans the wrong way.

The State of the Vatican City was created in 1929 by the signing of the Lateran Treaty, creating the smallest sovereign nation on earth (see box, page 17).

The border is sometimes obvious (the high stone wall that skirts the Vatican's northern, western and southern boundaries), sometimes obscure (the chain fence that separates St Peter's Square from the adjoining Piazza Pio XII) and occasionally – as in the case of extra-territorial buildings like the Castel Gandolfo in the surrounding hills – completely random.

Regardless, while the combined 0.44 square kilometres of the Vatican may be a world away from the sprawling Holy Roman Empire of the papacy's heyday, it is nonetheless a plot that the Church consolidates with due seriousness, resulting in a catalogue of domestic quirks that enchant and amuse visitors just as often as they infuriate its more secular neighbour.

The policy-making headquarters of Vatican City, as seen from the high dome of St Peter's Basilica.

When (Not) in Rome

The Vatican has its own post office (rumours that its service is significantly speedier than the Italian one leads to many Romans border-hopping to post their morning mail). It also has its own passports, with Vatican nationality – clocking in at 783 registered in July 2005 – conferred on cardinals, clergy and administrative workers within its walls, and usually taken straight back following termination of their employment.

There are also Vatican coins, stamps, a web domain (.va) and even a bank, this last boasting the only ATMs in the world to offer a service in Latin, the Vatican's official language. The Vatican economy, however, is non-commercial, relying instead on revenues from tourism (hardly insignificant, considering the museum queues that regularly run along its northern and eastern walls) and Peter's Pence, a voluntary contribution that

Vatican coins are popular with collectors, and are regularly reissued to feature the faces of various popes.

started with the Anglo-Saxons in the 8th century, although these days the Vatican accepts Amex, VISA, Diners Club and Mastercard, and contributions can be made via the website. Not all progress is bad progress, it would seem.

Meanwhile, those seeking their daily dose of headlines can pick up a copy of the Vatican newspaper, *L'Osservatore Romano*, which understandably sticks to a highly Catholicized version of world events, tracking the pope's movements and publishing his opinions alongside rambling papal documents that make the commodities section of the *Financial Times* read like a copy of *The Da Vinci Code*. Despite this, the paper is printed in seven languages and distributed in over 130 countries, while the official Vatican radio station, set up in 1931 and inaugurated by Pope Pius XI, broadcasts in almost 50 languages, with more than 200 journalists reporting from over 60 countries.

Rumours that the Vatican postal service is significantly quicker than its neighbour's causes many Romans to jump the border before posting their morning mail.

A Law unto Itself

Not all of the Vatican's domestic eccentricities sit so easily with the neighbouring Italian government. Its microscopic size, combined with the wealth of naïve tourists wandering within its borders, means that the Vatican's crime rate is the highest per capita of any nation on earth, and more than 20 times higher than in Italy itself. Despite this, Italian police and Carabinieri have no jurisdiction on Vatican grounds, which are instead patrolled by members of the instantly recognizable Swiss Guard, a Papal military force whose men have been laying down their lives in service of the pope since the 15th century.

Recruitment policies at the Swiss Guard are highly unorthodox, enrolling as it does only Swiss males between the ages of 19 and 30, the vast majority of whom are German-speaking (the minority of French speakers are reputed to be mocked and intimidated by their superior officers), and all of whom must be at least 5'9" tall. An unswerving allegiance to the pope is a given – any Swiss Guard must be ready at a moment's notice to hurl himself in front of a bullet with the pontiff's name on it – and therefore a strong Catholic faith is also mandatory.

For most people, Swiss Guards are embodied in their flamboyant technicolour uniforms – allegedly designed by Michelangelo, but leaning far more towards the ridiculous than the sublime.

Nor are Swiss Guards the only ones bound by an often unpopular dress code within the walls of the Vatican. Visit on a sweltering summer's day, and it can often seem as though there are as many tourists queuing for the Basilica as there are being turned away from the gates, their heads shaking in disbelief, their wide eyes incredulous. Some are wearing shorts, some tank tops, others are completely bare-chested, but all share a failure to see or adhere to the signs outlining Vatican clothing requirements: nothing ending above the knee, no bare shoulders and no bare feet.

Swiss Guards are embodied by their flamboyant and technicolour uniforms.

A permanent fixture in the Vatican, elaborately dressed Swiss Guards have been laying down their lives in the service of the pope for centuries.

The Popemobile

Few Vatican eccentricities are as iconic as the Popemobile – and it's not hard to see why. Combining the security of a military personnel carrier with the average crawl speed of a pre-war milkfloat, the world's favourite mode of papal transport has for

Flanked by security, Pope John Paul II greets the gathering crowds in his bullet-proof Popemobile.

decades been allowing the pontiff to weave his way through enormous crowds without taking so much as a step.

Various companies have produced popemobiles in the past, often one-off models coinciding with a much-publicized papal visit. For John Paul II's historic return to his native Poland in 1979, for example, a small Polish truck firm called Star produced a rudimentary Popemobile with a top speed of 6mph, while Land Rover built the vehicle used on his visit to England.

Following the attempted assassination of 1981 – when John Paul II was shot four times as he was driven around St Peter's Square – popemobiles have been fitted with bullet-proof windows and bomb-proof working parts, and high-profile companies have entered bidding wars to build the papal chariot. The current model is a modified Mercedes Benz ML Series with a full range of extras, but already Audi and BMW are rumoured to be lining up with proposals to construct the next one.

Inside a Papal Election

Upon the death or abdication of a pope, members of the College of Cardinals travel from around the world and convene in the Sistine Chapel, where the doors are closed and bolted and the solemn electoral process known as 'conclave' is set in motion.

It's ironic that the most sensitive and secretive of all Vatican rituals is also the one we know the most about. The development of technology has required a certain amount of fine-tuning by the authorities (the scrupulous search of the Sistine Chapel for electronic listening devices, for example), but the ceremony itself has changed little in the past 1,000 years.

First, the death of the pope must be verified by the Cardinal Carmelengo, who calls out the pope's Christian name – as opposed to his adopted papal name – three times. If there is no response, he takes possession of the deceased pope's Ring of the Fisherman – a unique gold ring featuring the

The papal election has changed very little in the past 1,000 years.

pontiff's name engraved around an image of St Peter – which, along with the seal used to authorize all papal documents, will later be destroyed in front of the cardinals. This practice was once believed to prevent forgery but is now retained for purely symbolic value. A six-day period then follows in which well-wishers may travel to the Vatican to pay their respects to the dead pope's body; after this comes the funeral, and then a nine-day period of mourning.

At the start of a conclave – which begins no more than 20 days after the death of the last pope – the cardinals take the Eucharist in St Peter's Basilica before making their way towards the Sistine Chapel on foot, singing the Veni Creator as they go. The Master of Papal Liturgical Celebrations then reads an oath of secrecy, which the cardinals confirm in turn, before ordering all unnecessary persons to leave and then closing and locking the chapel doors. Each cardinal may be accompanied by

*The death of a pope is the end of an era, but it also marks the beginning
of one of the most ancient and arcane ceremonies on earth.*

two attendant 'conclavists' (three if the
cardinal is ill), while a few priests remain
on hand to hear confessions,
as do doctors and housekeeping staff to
provide meals. No other communication
with the outside world is allowed.

The Casting of Ballots

On the first day of the electoral process, one ballot may be held in the afternoon; on all subsequent days, four ballots are held – two in the morning, two in the afternoon. Voting is periodically suspended following each set of seven unsuccessful ballots for prayer and speeches by increasingly high-ranking figures (first the Cardinal Deacon, then the senior Cardinal Priest and finally the senior Cardinal Bishop), all of them urging consensus and stressing the importance of ending the period known as *sede vacante* ('vacant seat'). If none manage to resolve the stalemate, the cardinals may then vote to change the rules – perhaps by eliminating all but the top two candidates, or reducing the majority needed to swing the election in a particular candidate's favour.

Smoke Signals

If no majority is reached during a papal vote, the ballot papers are burned in a purpose-built chimney along with a chemical that causes black smoke to pour forth from the roof of the Sistine Chapel (damp straw was traditionally used, but proved unreliable); if a consensus has been reached, the ballots are burned on their own, with the chapel bells ringing simultaneously to herald the coming of the new pope – and to prevent any confusion on the off-chance that the smoke isn't white enough to be obvious.

Following the 2005 election of Pope Benedict XVI, however, the peal of bells was delayed by ten minutes. Some speculated that this was due to a problem caused by having to disable an electronic system normally used to ring in the hours automatically (it was approaching 6pm); others claim that the official in charge, overwhelmed with excitement, simply forgot. Either way, on a day that also saw the inside of the Sistine Chapel fill with acrid smoke as the burning of the ballots went awry, it was proof that even a ceremony as ancient and well-established as the conclave isn't immune to the occasional error.

The process for all ballots, however, remains the same: cardinals are given slips of paper on which are written the words 'Eligo in Summum Pontificem' ('I elect as Supreme Pontiff'); after writing down nothing more than the name of their preferred candidate (the vote is completely anonymous), the cardinals take their slips to one of three randomly selected Scrutineers, who then shake, remove and count the ballots. Assuming the number of slips corresponds to the number of cardinals present (if not, they must be burned and the election recast), the names on the ballots are read aloud and written down before being double-checked by a team of three Revisers (like the Scrutineers, drawn by lots at the beginning of each new vote and then dismissed immediately after it).

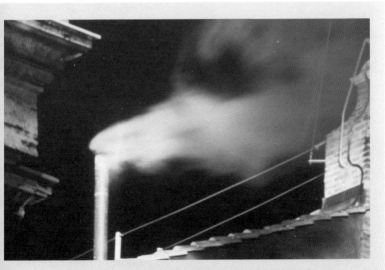

White smoke pours forth from the chimney of the Sistine Chapel, a sign that the assembled cardinals have decided on a new pope.

The Roots of a Ritual

*The Episcopal Palace at Viterbo, site of the first conclave. In 1270,
its roof was actually removed in an effort to speed up the papal election.*

The ceremonial conclave dates back to the year 1059. In an attempt to counter the increasing politicization of papal elections due to interference by the crowned heads of Europe, Pope Nicholas II decreed that only cardinals would bear responsibility for choosing the pontifical candidate, which would then be presented to the clergy and the laity for consent; in 1139, the Synod of the Lateran removed the need for this consent, tightening up the whole process even further.

Bread and water was the only sustenance provided to the cardinals who deliberated for almost three years during the conclave convened to replace Pope Clement IV.

It wasn't until a century later, however, that the forced seclusion of the cardinals came into effect, giving rise to the term 'conclave' (from *con clavis*, Latin for 'with a key'). This was the result of a notoriously drawn-out papal election following the death of Clement IV in 1268, when the cardinals dithered for no less than two years and nine days, after which point the city authorities ushered them into the Episcopal Palace in the city of Viterbo and locked the gates behind them. Still no decision was forthcoming, and so the cardinals were sent nothing but bread and water for sustenance. When even this failed to yield a result, the local people set to work removing the roof above the cardinals' heads – a desperate measure, but one which resulted in the cardinals very quickly electing Gregory X as pope, thus ending a *sede vacante* of almost three years.

The Vatican versus the Media

Accusations of Vatican mind control are never more vehement than over its policy on freedom of the press, which to this day seems as closed and calculated as that of a paranoid dictator state.

More than 1,500 people died when Hurricane Katrina overwhelmed the New Orleans levees in August 2005. Nine months earlier, nearly 200,000 people were killed by the Boxing Day tsunami that annihilated Southeast Asia.

Yet the death of one man, on 2 April 2005, seemed to generate more news coverage across Europe than both of these events. Most media outlets ran almost identical versions of the same story. His last words, they said, were in his native Polish: 'Let me go to the house of the Father.' Several close aides were present, they told us, as were a handful of Polish nuns, and mass had just been celebrated at his bedside when he finally slipped away. And yet, of the roughly 6,000 journalists that would later report such details, only one could claim to have been in attendance at the passing of Pope John Paul II.

His name is Dr Joaquin Navarro-Valls, a distinguished scientist, linguist and high-ranking member of Opus Dei. Until 2006, Navarro-Valls was also Director of the Vatican Press Office, a position he took up in 1984. In that role, he was more than just the pope's official spokesman: he was also the conduit through which the public viewed the papacy, and as such he decided exactly which side of the papacy the public saw.

What happens inside the Vatican stays inside the Vatican…

The official line in all cases has been the hard line: what happens inside the Vatican's walls, it seems, stays inside those walls, and roaming journalists are as unwelcome as members of the municipal police.

*Until 2006, Dr Joaquin Navarro-Valls was the highly influential
and often controversial director of the Vatican Press Office.*

Publish and Be Damned

The Vatican refuses point blank to play ball with the press, but this isn't a new phenomenon. As far back as 1832, in his papal encyclical *Miraro Vos* (On Liberalism and Religious Indifferentism), the ultraconservative Pope Gregory XVI condemned freedom of conscience as 'a false and absurd concept'. His successor,

Pope Pius IX, saw press freedoms as 'intrinsically evil' – no doubt a factor that encouraged him to convene the First Vatican Council in 1869 and establish the notion of papal infallibility. The following year, the newspaper *Unità Cattolica* published an editorial commending the merits of his decision: 'The infallible pope must counteract and cure the prevailing abuses of unbridled freedom of the press... Every day the pope can teach, condemn and define dogma, and Catholics will never be permitted to question his decisions.'

Pope Pius IX described freedom of the press as 'intrinsically evil'.

Those that did question, meanwhile, soon felt the full force of the Church's anger. In 1928, a Jesuit priest named Charles Mullaly gave an interview to *America* magazine in which he proudly outlined Catholic methods for intimidation and suppression of the press. As an example, he cited the suspicious death of a young girl at a Washington-based Catholic home run by the Sisters of the Good Shepherd, after which a DC newspaper published a slew of letters from concerned parents demanding an immediate independent investigation.

The Catholic Society's response, instead of stirring up further controversy by mounting a defence of the sisters, was to target the business rather than the editorial department of the offending paper, preaching a boycott from the pulpit and persuading church-going merchants who advertised in its pages to threaten terminating their contracts unless such behaviour ceased immediately. Circulation dropped by 40% in just two weeks, and the matter was swiftly dropped.

This was achieved without a single memorandum or long-winded committee meeting: all that was required was a

suitably threatening name ('The Washington Truth Society', in this case), a convincing letterhead and a couple of well-connected members to motivate the many Catholics in positions of power across the capital. 'In any city of the United States," stated Mullaly, "one zealous pastor with two or three active laymen, together with a legal advisor, could form a Truth Society that would batter to pieces bigotry when found in the pages of any local newspaper.'

Over the decades, the media has operated in constant fear of infuriating the papacy.

Bury the Hardest Truth First

It's not just local newspapers that are subject to Vatican media manipulation. Catholic views on family planning have been well-known since Pius XI's 1930 encyclical *Casti Connubii* ('On Christian Marriage'), in which he blasted contraception as 'a crime against nature'. It wasn't until 20 November 1975, however, almost three years after the US legalization of abortion, that the Church set up its Pastoral Plan for Pro-Life Activities, which immediately began lobbying powerful Catholics on Capitol Hill to help reverse the trend.

Six days later, President Ford was presented with a National Security Memorandum (NSSM 200), which drew attention to the terrifying consequences of international overpopulation. Its recommendations included a worldwide campaign, led by the US, to promote the importance of small families and increase the availability of abortions and contraception, in an attempt to prevent what it called 'a current danger of the highest magnitude'. It was almost certainly the single most important investigation ever made into population control, yet thanks to pressure from Catholic insiders (and President Ford's desire to court the

Catholic vote) it was immediately buried. When the report was finally made public, in 1989, the world population crisis had spiralled further out of control.

The Vatican media machine, it seems, operates on two levels. On the one

hand, there are people like Joaquin Navarro-Valls ready with an official line to rebut a scandal like the one surrounding the Swiss Guard Murders of 1998, or to shed a tear to show how moving it was to be at the deathbed of John Paul II. What happens inside the Vatican, stays inside the Vatican – but it doesn't end there. As the disappearance of the NSSM report goes to show, the Vatican's official line often extends far beyond its walls, affecting world decisions and changing the lives of millions on a regular basis.

The Vatican is a political as well as a religious body, and its influence regularly affects international policy making as far away as Capitol Hill.

Insider Trading

The Vatican Press Office may be a far
from flawless source of information,
but things are a great deal better than
in the days before the Second Vatican
Council (1962-1965), when there was
no press office at all. In his book
Anatomy of the Vatican, Paul Hoffman
recalls his tenure as a Vatican reporter
for the *New York Times*, when he and
other journalists were forced to buy
information from unreliable insiders.

One of these was Riccardo Galeazzi-Lisi,
the bogus papal doctor who would
later so horribly bungle the embalming
of Pope Pius XII; another was Emilio
Pucci, a former cardinal secretary of
state, who would rattle out regular
typewritten bulletins of important
Vatican events for paying customers
(and personally phone those who paid a
little more).

Pucci's reports were riddled with holes
and translational errors: Hoffman
recalls one incident where he excitedly
chased up a story that the Archbishop
of New York was making a pastoral trip
to the Middle East, only to find that he
was actually travelling to the American
Midwest. Pucci was later denounced as

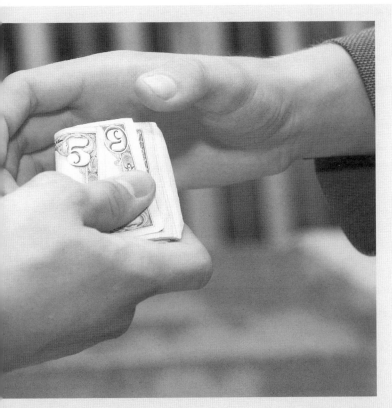

an informant to OVRA, Mussolini's secret
police, although Hoffman was convinced
they were receiving nothing more than
his regular bulletins.

*Journalists are often
forced to resort to buying
information when writing
stories on the notoriously
secretive Vatican.*

A Man's World

With a mistrust of feminine wiles underpinning the Bible and a simmering machismo ingrained in the execution of Church affairs, it's a wonder that even a handful of women have been written into the history of the Vatican.

When the Vatican's 'Letter to the Bishops of the Catholic Church on the Collaboration of Men and Women in the Church and the World' was published in 2004, it sent the collective blood pressure of the women's rights movement sky high. The document stressed that motherhood was the 'key element of women's identities', and slammed the 'lethal effects' of feminism for undermining the traditional two-parent family system and making 'homosexuality and heterosexuality virtually equivalent'.

It's little wonder that those few women who left their mark on Vatican history tend to have been written into legend as a result.

The author of such controversial claims? None other than Cardinal Joseph Ratzinger, who one year later succeeded John Paul II as Pope Benedict XVI.

As a result of their marginalized place within the Church, it's little wonder that those few women who left their mark on Vatican history tend to have been written into legend. Often their infamy is due to exactly those same 'feminine wiles' of which the Church is so suspicious: the many mistresses and prostitutes engaged and entertained by Pope Alexander VI, for example, or Donna Olimpia Maidalchini-Pamphili, who used her influence as sister-in-law to Pope Innocent X for personal gain within the Vatican (her son was made a cardinal), before abandoning the stricken pope on his deathbed in 1655 and refusing to pay for his funeral.

Nuns have always embodied the Vatican's view of a woman's place in society: virginal and devout.

Daughters of Christ

Not all women's names are scored aggressively in the Vatican's bad books. Indeed, many are famous for having displayed an intense spirituality and devotion to the Church that exceeded that of most popes. One example is Countess Matilda of Tuscany, who in the 11th century supported Pope Gregory VII during his cataclysmic schism with the Holy Roman Emperor and became the first woman interred in the Vatican as a result. Or the ascetic St Catherine of Sienna, who in 1377 did what no educated statesman had been able to do and persuaded Gregory XI to move the embattled papacy from Avignon back to Rome, where she then spent the rest of her life in the court of Pope Urban VI.

Never before have saintliness and sinfulness made such comfortable bedfellows as in Bernini's sculpture.

Queen Christina of Sweden, meanwhile, abdicated in 1654 to practise openly her previously secret Catholicism, taking on a new name (Maria Christina Alexandra) and moving to Rome, where she became the centre of society thanks to her wealth and fame (although her refusal to adhere to many of the less sociable aspects of her religion infuriated Pope Alexander VII). She left her vast library to the papacy following her death, and was afforded the rare privilege of being buried in the crypt of St Peter's.

And yet, perhaps only one woman has achieved a legendary status through both her devout spirituality and implied sexuality – and she's not really a woman at all. The seemingly orgasmic euphoria on display in Bernini's sculpture *The Ecstasy of St Theresa* (1652), housed in the Santa Maria della Vittoria in Rome, is based on the life of a nun who described her encounter with a beautiful angel with a long fiery spear, who 'appeared to me to be thrusting it at times into my heart, and to pierce my very entrails'. Never before have saintliness and sinfulness made such comfortable bedfellows.

Bernini's sculpture, The Ecstasy of St Theresa, *mixes the sacred and the seemingly sinful in its ambiguous portrayal of one woman's spiritual bliss.*

They Dare Not Speak Her Name

Few historical figures have rattled the chains of the Church like the legendary Pope Joan – the female pontiff now largely agreed to be a character of folklore, but whose spirit nonetheless haunts the papacy to this day.

Many versions of the same story exist, although the most popular – written by a 13th century Vatican chaplain called Martin Troppau – alleges that Joan was actually an English lady who adopted male clothes and the name 'John of Mainz' before heading to Athens, where she astonished scholars with her unprecedented academic ability.

She then moved to Rome to teach science, attracting such attention that she was eventually elected pope in 855 AD, but thereafter became pregnant by one of her attendants and ended up unveiling her femininity by unexpectedly giving birth on a papal procession through the city. She died almost immediately, although whether during childbirth or from subsequent stoning is unclear.

The source of the legend is equally obscure: some say it stemmed from a cynical slur on the effeminate weakness of Pope John VIII in dealing with invading Saracens in the 9th century; others from a monument to an unidentified woman discovered in a side-street near the Colosseum.

Either way, well-wishers maintain a tribute there to this day, and while papal processions do avoid the spot, many argue that this is simply because it is so narrow.

Another rumour claimed that subsequently elected popes were made to sit naked on a marble seat with a hole in the bottom, under which a committee of cardinals would peer, in turn, and confirm 'Testiculos habet et bene pendentes' ('He has testicles, and they dangle nicely'), although this is universally believed to be hokum of the highest order.

Pope Joan unveiled her femininity by unexpectedly giving birth on a procession.

Joan Pope of Rome 856

A Woman Pope (*as History doth tell*)
In High Procession *once in Labour fell,*
And was Deliver'd *of a* Bastard Son ; ——
Whence Rome *some call* The Whore of Babylon.

A depiction of
the mythical
Pope Joan giving
birth during a
papal procession.
The story is
widely believed
to be little more
than that.

'Mother' Pasqualina

No woman of the cloth has generated hostility in the Vatican like Pope Pius XII's inseparable German housekeeper. The daughter of a Bavarian farmer, Sister Pasqualina (the title 'Mother' was never officially ordained) met the then Monsignor Eugenio Pacelli while he was recovering from serious illness at her nunnery in Switzerland. She made such an impression that Pacelli requested her direct transfer to Munich, where she began work as his housekeeper – highly unorthodox, given Pasqualina's reputedly radiant beauty and the fact that Pacelli was 18 years her senior. Rumours of an affair began circulating, but these were quickly quashed by a formal investigation ordered by Pacelli himself.

The pair then moved to Berlin, where Pacelli was serving as papal diplomat to the German Reich, and thence to Rome, where Pasqualina entered the Sistine Chapel as Pacelli's assistant in the conclave

Most Vatican insiders despised Pasqualina and her hold over Pius XII.

Pope Pius XII raised more than a few eyebrows when he employed a young, attractive nun as his papal housekeeper.

that led to his election as pope. Following this, she became a permanent presence in the Vatican as the papal housekeeper, ruling over a small palace of her own and accumulating such influence over Pius that she was believed to have been able to get even cardinals ordained.

She became swamped with letters from people seeking money or a job in the Vatican, and fawned upon by officials unable to secure a direct papal audience. Despite this, however, most Vatican insiders despised her – especially towards the end of Pius' life, when she was seen as directly encouraging the holy visions and visitations that many saw as the onset of senility.

Following his death, she was ordered to stay away from the Vatican after it was discovered that she had burned two bags of documents on the deceased pope's orders – a fact she freely admitted, arguing that 'a pope's orders must be carried out'. No one knows to this day what the documents actually contained.

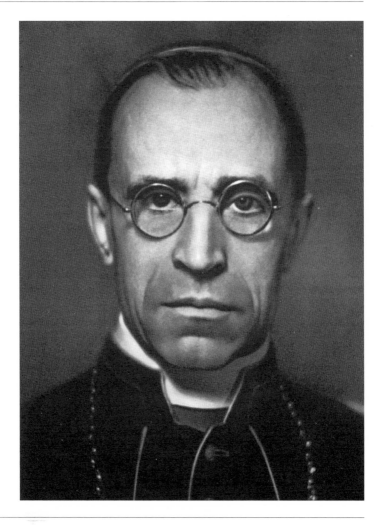

PART FOUR
Death and the Vatican

The Catholic authorities who run the Vatican would have you believe that death only ever comes calling at the Vatican due to entirely natural causes – but this is often not the case. The history of the Church is liberally peppered with episodes of foul play, feverish conspiracy and downright murder dating back centuries, as this section reveals.

First under the spotlight is Pope Alexander VI, whose reign embodied the lowest moral ebb of a spiritually corrupt Church, where murders went unpunished on a daily basis, many of them instigated by the pontiff himself. Alexander eventually fell foul of his own favoured method of assassination – a slow and painful poison – and so it seems only appropriate that our next chapter deals with the untimely ends of popes throughout the ages.

Murder, the mafia and papal corruption – the Vatican's shady past is filled with scandal and controversy.

On a more gruesome note, we then look into one of the most embarrassing episodes in the history of the modern Vatican: namely, the botched embalming of Pope Pius XII by a doctor who turned the traditional funerary rites into a surreal carnival of stomach-turning disasters.

There then follows a retelling of the tragic 1982 murder of the Italian banker Roberto Calvi, whose shady financial dealings with the Vatican bank led him into a deadly triangle of Church insiders, freemasons and fearsome mafia types, all of whom contributed to his undignified end, swinging beneath a London bridge.

Finally, we investigate a murder that shocked the world. In 1998, a member of the Swiss Guard brutally killed both his superior officer and the man's wife in paranoid rage – or, at least, that was the Vatican's official version of events...

*Alexander VI (eating) alongside his illegitimate children
Cesare and Lucrezia Borgia: a 16th century 'axis of evil'.*

The Reign of Terror

No single pope has left a stain on the history of the Vatican like Alexander VI (1492-1503), who ruled with such nepotism, despotism and decadence that to this day the very mention of his name causes many in the Church to shake their heads in shame.

It's hard to believe that a man who reputedly committed his first murder at the age of 12 could end up as head of the Holy See, but then Rodrigo Borgia won the papal election with the same moral vacuity that characterized his reign, sending four mules loaded with silver to his closest competitor, Cardinal Ascanio Sforza, to help swing the vote in his favour.

From that point on, things only got worse. Alexander had sired no fewer than ten illegitimate children with various mistresses, and as pope he engaged in a campaign of ruthless nepotism, elevating many to positions of power (his son Cesare was made Archbishop of Valencia while still a student of 17), and setting up his mistresses in smart houses across

To this day, many in the papacy squirm at the very mention of Alexander VI, whose litany of papal abuses was seemingly without end.

It's hard to believe that a man who reputedly committed his first murder aged 12 could end up as pope.

Rome – one, Giulia Farnese, was even used as a model for the Virgin Mary in a recently rediscovered fresco for the papal apartments.

As Alexander's power grew, so did his greed, and the Borgia coat of arms – a rampant red bull against a field of gold – became increasingly appropriate. Before long, wealthy cardinals were being imprisoned and executed on trumped-up charges, simply so Alexander could get his hands on their property. Rome was plunged into a period of unprecedented darkness, its streets crawling with prostitutes and murders going unpunished, while the pope occupied himself with alcohol-fuelled banquets that invariably turned into orgies. It was a scandal the likes of which the Vatican had never seen, and one from which it would never fully recover.

The notoriously lecherous Borgia pope, here depicted enjoying the performance of a dancing girl.

The Devil's Own

If Alexander VI was directing the action across Europe at the turn of the 15th century, then it was to his immediate family that he gave many of the leading roles – and there was no actor more versatile than his illegitimate daughter, Lucrezia.

Alexander's manipulation of Lucrezia's hand in marriage started early: she had been betrothed twice by the age of eleven, although on both occasions her father called off the engagements. Such indecisiveness came to a head when Alexander became pope and started seeking allies to consolidate his claim. The first of these was Giovanni Sforza, a powerful Milanese noble to whom Alexander hurriedly married off Lucrezia, but who soon proved to be a less beneficial connection than had first been hoped. Alexander requested a divorce, which Sforza refused; the pope then ruled the union invalid, arguing that his son-in-law had been unable to consummate the marriage, and Sforza was forced to sign the annulment papers – and a confession of impotence – in front of witnesses.

Sforza was understandably bitter: when Lucrezia became pregnant around the time of their separation, he claimed that the child belonged to her brother, Cesare.

Sforza also accused his ex-wife of indulging in incestuous relations with her father, the pope – accusations to which many historians impart some credibility.

Corruption and depravity clearly ran in the Borgia blood. Pictured here are the illicit children of Pope Alexander VI, the despotic Cesare and his sister Lucrezia, who were rumoured to have indulged in an incestuous relationship that led to the birth of a son – although some speculate that the child was fathered by none other than the pope himself.

Regardless of what inspired such claims, there was certainly a bond between brother and sister that went beyond mere sibling protectiveness. Lucrezia soon entered into another marriage of convenience – this time with the dashing Alfonso of Aragon – but Cesare, who received severe facial scarring as a result of smallpox and had taken to wearing a mask, became jealous of her new husband's good looks, ordering his men to attack him on a visit to Rome and then having the young duke strangled while he recovered in bed.

The motive may have been envy, but there was certainly a political aspect to the murder: as with Sforza's before him, Alfonso's alliance was proving less than beneficial, and Alexander had new plans for his daughter. Not long after, Lucrezia was married off to Alphonso d'Este, Prince of Ferrara, and it was with him that she spent the rest of her life, putting behind her the dark days spent in the court of her father (where she is rumoured to have worn a ring filled with poison for dinner party assassinations) and learning to play a new role – that of the worldly Renaissance duchess.

A Welcome End

Alexander's passing, when it finally came, was slow and excruciatingly painful: contemporary sources describe the pontiff's face going the colour of wine, his stomach swelling and turning to liquid, and his skin peeling off. Following his death, the body was exhibited to the Roman people in a strangely accelerated state of decomposition (his tongue grotesquely engorged, his frozen mouth foaming); by now the corpse had swollen so much that attendants had to jump on it to force it into the coffin, at which point it began releasing sulphurous gases from every orifice.

All the signs pointed to poisoning: the most despotic pope in history, who murdered left, right and centre those who stood in the

The Ballet of the Chestnuts

The list of amoral acts committed by Alexander VI is almost without end, but there is one event so surreal in its debauchery that it has come to define the level to which the papacy sank during his reign. On the evening of 30 October 1501, the pope held a supper in his papal apartments that quickly turned into the wildest of all his parties.

Once the tables had been cleared, the fifty most beautiful prostitutes in Rome entered the hall and began dancing with the guests, before being made to remove their clothes and crawl naked around the floor on all fours picking up scattered chestnuts – an act which led to it being remembered as the Ballet of the Chestnuts.

After this, the orgy began, with guests encouraged to have sex with as many of the prostitutes as possible while the pope looked proudly on. Servants were at hand to keep a record of the couplings, and after it was finished the pope took to the floor, handing out prizes to those men who had managed to copulate with the most courtesans. The measure of a man, according to Alexander, was his virility – to which end, he must certainly have held himself in quite high regard.

way of his Machiavellian plans, had quite literally been given a taste of his own medicine. It was hardly surprising, given the number of enemies he had made both in and out of the Vatican, and, for many, his death didn't come a moment too soon.

The priests of St Peter's Basilica were understandably reluctant to take the body for burial, only doing so when forced to by the authorities (just four prelates attended the funeral), and then hurriedly removing and re-interring it in another, smaller church. His successor, Pope Pius III, went so far as to forbid the saying of mass for the sanctity of Alexander's soul, noting that 'it is blasphemous to pray for the damned'.

The humble chestnut was a thorn in the side of the Vatican in more ways than one, playing a central role in Alexander VI's depraved Ballet of the Chestnuts – an episode that haunts the papacy to this very day.

Assassination in the Vatican

Alexander VI's death by poisoning in 1503 was highly unpleasant, but hardly unusual: throughout history, the increasing politicization of the Vatican meant that maverick popes regularly met with untimely ends.

John Paul II is shot as his open-topped popemobile traverses St Peter's Square in 1981.

John VIII is believed to have been the first pope assassinated (poisoned and then clubbed to death by his own followers in 882 AD), but he was certainly not the last: many more followed, including John X (suffocated with a pillow in 928 AD) and Benedict VI (strangled by a priest in 974 AD).

The 20th century witnessed at least three attempts on the lives of popes (the attempted stabbing of Paul VI by a surrealist painter at Manila Airport in 1970, and the two attempted assassinations of John Paul II in 1981 and 1982), while more may have gone unrecorded. What is most unsettling, however, is the seemingly peaceful passing of two popes from causes that may have been anything but natural...

PIUS XI

In 1939, as Hitler was consolidating his stranglehold over Europe, an elderly Pope Pius XI became increasingly concerned with the meteoric rise of fascism and the threat it posed to ethnic minorities. He set to work preparing a bluntly worded speech denouncing fascism both at home and abroad. Alas, twenty-four hours before he was due to deliver it, he was found dead, apparently of a failing heart. The text of his bold speech had miraculously disappeared, and has never been recovered.

Not long after, rumours of foul play began circulating. These were based on a sensational claim in the personal diaries of a respected French cardinal named Eugene Tisserant, who noted that Pius had been given an injection on the day of his death by one Dr Francesco Petacci, the Vatican's chief medical practitioner and the father of none other than the long-term mistress of Mussolini himself.

While the conspiracy theory that Pius XI was murdered on the orders of Mussolini is not widely accepted, his sudden death, just hours before making a speech that could have changed the course of the 20th century, has understandably raised a great number of eyebrows – especially in the light of his successor Pius XII's perceived support for the Third Reich. There's little doubt that the Vatican was under the sway of pro-fascist forces at the start of WWII; the question is whether or not they murdered one of their own – and that question seems unlikely to be answered any time soon.

Some speculate that Pope Pius XI was assassinated to prevent him from making a speech condemning the rise of fascism.

JOHN PAUL I

Pius XI wasn't the last pope of the 20th century to have his legacy tarnished with rumours of an untimely demise. Indeed, demises don't get much more untimely than that of John Paul I, whose death, on 28 September 1978, came just 33 days after his election as pope.

Official reports of the event were fragmented and conflicting. One stated that the body had been found in the papal bedroom at 4.30am; another placed the time of the discovery at 5.30am. One said that the pope had felt ill the previous night but had decided against calling a doctor; another said that he had been conversing cheerfully with his secretaries before dinner, and showed no signs of any ailment. Nor were the causes of death any more consistent. One report said that he'd died of a heart attack, although a leading cardinal named Jean-Marie Villot insisted that he'd accidentally overdosed on his coronary medication, Effortil – a controversial claim, as it opened the pope up to accusations of suicide.

This was hard to verify, however, as the bottle disappeared from the scene –

as did the pope's glasses and slippers. In his book, *In God's Name*, David Yallop suggested that these were removed because they would have shown traces of vomiting – a symptom of digitalis poisoning, which would also have accounted for the expression of twisted agony on the face of a man once known as the 'Smiling Pope'.

But why would anyone want John Paul dead? Simply put, the new pope was threatening to shake up the Vatican in an unprecedented fashion.

He had already disposed of the ancient coronation ceremony and broken with tradition by taking two papal names instead of one (the first pope ever to do so); now he was promising to investigate the internal Vatican bank scandal, clean out the nepotistic 'Milan Mafia' of his predecessor Paul VI, ease the Catholic line on abortion and contraception, and possibly even disband the Jesuit order for a second time. The truth is that there were so many viable motives for his murder that the real culprit, if there is one, may never be found.

Pope John Paul I at
his inauguration,
held on 23
September 1978.
Just five days after
this picture was
taken, the new
pope was found
dead in his
bedroom under
highly suspicious
circumstances.

The Third Secret of Fatima

While serving time in an Italian jail for his attempted assassination of John Paul II in 1981, the Turkish dissident Mehmet Ali Agca became obsessed with what was widely known as the Third Secret of Fatima.

In 1917, in the Portuguese village of Aljustrel, near Fatima, three peasant children claimed to have received repeated visitations from the Virgin Mary, who imparted to them three secrets: the first was a gruelling vision of Hell, the second an insight into how to save souls from eternal damnation by converting the world to Christianity,

Many believe that the real Third Secret of Fatima remains buried to this day.

while the third was considered so sensitive that it was to be kept under wraps until 1940.

The Vatican, however, decided to keep hold of it for much longer, all the while dropping hints of its seriousness and power (in 1980, John Paul II equated it to reading that 'the oceans will inundate continents, and millions of people will die suddenly in a few minutes'). And yet, when the Third Secret was finally revealed on 26 July 2000, it turned out to be a long-winded allegory featuring an angel with a flaming sword, a city half in ruins and the Holy Father being shot with bullets and arrows at the foot of a cross.

According to the Vatican, this was a prophetic vision of Ali Agca's assassination attempt in 1981, which they noted had occurred on 13 May, the Feast Day of Fatima. Beyond this, however, the link was tenuous to say the least, and many believe that the real Third Secret of Fatima remains buried to this day.

Of the three
secrets said
to have been
imparted by
the Virgin
Mary to three
Portuguese
peasant
children in
1917, one is
rumoured to
remain under
wraps in
the Vatican.

A Very Grave Mistake

Pope Pius XII's death was as controversial as his life, and it was all thanks to one man: a quack doctor named Riccardo Galeazzi-Lisi, who bungled the embalming of the papal body so badly that it haunted the Vatican for years to come.

Despite being certified as nothing more than an eye specialist, Riccardo Galeazzi-Lisi, who had already known Pius for several years when he was elected pope in 1939, nevertheless managed to insinuate himself completely into Vatican life – first as the pope's personal doctor, then as arch physician to the papacy as a whole.

He even insisted that everyone in the Vatican address him as 'professor', although it was a title he'd never officially earned, and a medical prodigy he most certainly was not.

He had everyone in the Vatican address him as 'professor', even though he had never earned the title.

He was, however, a Vatican informant, passing inside information on to a number of paying customers, including journalists at both *The New York Times* and Reuters; as the elderly pope's condition deteriorated, the latter was even given a direct line to the doctor's office via a dramatic red telephone, although most clients simply handed over unmarked envelopes stuffed with cash in exchange for the scoop on the Vatican's internal affairs.

None of this came out until after Pius' death; if it had, Galeazzi-Lisi would never have been allowed to look upon, let alone administer to, the dead body of his beloved pontiff. As it was, when Pius finally passed away in the Castel Gandolfo on 9 October 1958, the doctor insisted on personally seeing to the embalming procedure, and the Vatican authorities agreed. It was a decision they would regret for the rest of their lives.

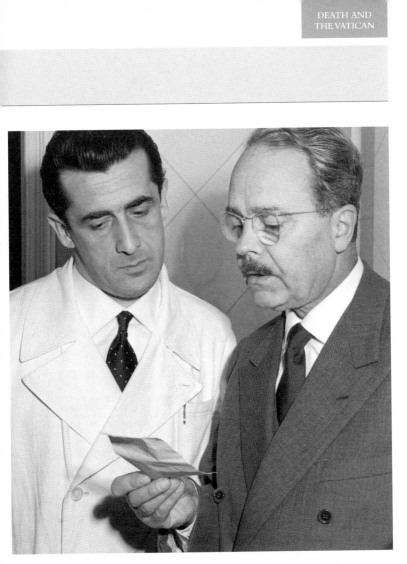

Riccardo Galeazzi-Lisi (right) was a largely incompetent eye doctor who somehow ended up as Pope Pius XII's personal physician. His botched embalming of the late pontiff led to one of the most embarrassing episodes in the history of the modern Vatican.

9–11 October: Signs of Decay

Things began to go wrong almost immediately. Galeazzi-Lisi and his personal assistant remained at work behind closed doors for two days before the body was deemed ready for transferral to St Peter's, where it would be exhibited to the public before burial. The hearse itself was the cause of much embarrassment – an unfeasibly tacky carriage featuring four stone angels and a three-tiered papal crown, all of it swaying unnervingly as it rattled along the Roman cobbles – but it was as the body was being shuffled into the Lateran Basilica for the funereal rites that the assembled mourners received their first real shock.

Closer inspection revealed that the coffin had split, a result of the body fermenting in the warm weather.

A loud crack echoed across the gathering. At first, officials believed a gunman had infiltrated the ceremony, but closer inspection revealed that the coffin had actually split, a result of the body fermenting in the unseasonably warm October weather and filling the enclosed space with necrotic gases. Church officials rushed through the rest of the ceremony before bundling the ruptured coffin back onto the hearse.

Galeazzi-Lisi was called to account for his embalming procedures. The doctor insisted that his method was based on an all-natural, ancient Egyptian formula that would keep the body in a pristine condition for more than a century without the need for chemicals or invasive surgery. All it entailed, he said, was encasing the corpse in a cellophane bag along with a precise combination of aromatic herbs; he just needed a little more time to perfect the procedure. Alas, time didn't help.

11–13 October: From Bad to Worse

The doctor and his assistant worked through the night in St Peter's, stopping only at 7am, when the doors were opened and the first mourners arrived. Initially, nothing seemed amiss, but as the morning wore on and the temperature rose, the deceased pope's face turned a distressing shade of green, while a foul smell began emanating from the body. Horrified officials called an exhausted Galeazzi-Lisi, who was once again made to work through the night. Alas, the next day was no better: the pope's face started to show large purplish blotches, and the same lingering smell pervaded the basilica's immense interior.

The last rites were hurriedly dispensed and the coffin rushed into the crypt beneath St Peter's, thus bringing to an end one the most embarrassing episodes in the history of the modern Catholic Church. Things came to a head days later, however, when a newspaper published a photograph of the dying pope taken by none other than Galeazzi-Lisi himself.

On 21 October, less than two weeks after the pope's passing, Galeazzi-Lisi was stripped of his titles and forbidden from setting foot within the Vatican ever again – the first and only time such a penalty has been imposed.

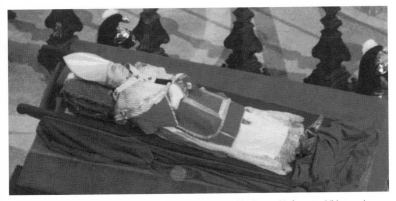

The smell that hung over Pius XII's corpse was awful, and the blotches on his face are visible even here.

The Cadaver Synod

Pius XII's wasn't the first rotting corpse to embarrass the Vatican; at the end of the 9th century, the papacy orchestrated an event so grotesque that it turned even stomachs galvanized by the hardships of the Middle Ages.

When Stephen VI was elected pope in 896 AD, it was largely thanks to his sponsors, the powerful Spoleto family, who had fallen out with Church authorities when the former Pope Formosus refused to crown one of their own as co-ruler of the Holy Roman Emperor. As a result, one of Stephen's first acts as pope – under pressure from the Spoletans, obviously – was to exhume the remains of Pope Formosus, clad them in papal garments and tie them to a chair, before putting them on trial in what became known as the Cadaver Synod.

Nor did his grisly theatrics end there. The corpse, inevitably enough, was found guilty, after which it had three of its fingers cut off before being buried in the clothes of a peasant; it was then re-exhumed and thrown in the River Tiber. Not long after, rumours began circulating that Formosus' body had washed up on its banks and begun performing miracles.

It was all too much for the horrified Roman populace, which demanded so vehemently that Stephen be deposed that the Spoletans eventually relented, imprisoning him and then having him strangled in his cell. His successor, Theodore II, annulled the verdict of the Synod and brought back Formosus' body (which had turned up in the harbour town of Porto), clothing it in full papal regalia and re-interring it in the family tomb.

The decaying remains of Pope
Formosus were dug up and dressed in
papal regalia, and then put on trial by
his successor, Stephen VI.

The Bizarre End of God's Banker

In 1982, a symbolic killing shattered the Vatican's image of financial inscrutability, dragging it into a murky world populated by mafia insiders, murderous freemasons and shameless money grabbers.

The disgraced banker Roberto Calvi (centre), who would later be found swinging from a rope beneath London's Blackfriars Bridge.

Agatha Christie herself couldn't have come up with a more atmospheric opening scene. At 7.30am, on 18 June 1982, a postman discovered the body of a man swinging from beneath Blackfriars Bridge in central London, his pockets stuffed with stones and roughly $15,000 in foreign currencies. A few phone calls later, the Metropolitan Police confirmed that this was the corpse of Roberto Calvi, the missing chairman of the Italian Banco Ambrosiano, which had recently collapsed with debts of up to $1.5 billion.

A seemingly clear-cut verdict of suicide was recorded, and the case closed – until 1998, that is, when protests from Calvi's family resulted in the exhumation of the body and a complex reconstruction of the crime scene, leading to a verdict of murder finally being filed in 2002, 20 years after the event itself.

It's hard to believe that such compelling evidence was overlooked the first time round: the injuries to Calvi's neck, for example, were inconsistent with hanging; he hadn't touched the stones

Protests from Calvi's family resulted in the exhumation of the body and a complex reconstruction of the crime scene.

in his pockets; and there was no rust on his shoes from the scaffolding that he would have needed to climb in order to reach the bridge.

Various underworld figures have since been indicted over the murder, including Licio Gelli, the head of Propoganda Due (P2), a masonic lodge that played a key part in the Banco Ambrosiano collapse. Tellingly, members of P2 refer to themselves as *frati neri* or 'black friars', a sinister nod towards the location of the murder.

It was potential Vatican involvement, however, that caused the most scandal, and which led to Roberto Calvi's nickname: God's Banker.

The Last Temptation

The collapse of Banco Ambrosiano shattered the Vatican's whiter-than-white reputation by revealing an enormous network of illegitimate investments traceable to the Vatican Institute for Religious Works (IOR).

Despite operating inside a non-commercial economy, the IOR had built up assets of almost $1 billion by the mid-50s. By the late 60s, the lion's share of decisions were being made by a Sicilian mafia associate and P2 mason named Michael Sindona, who began laundering money between his own Banca Privata and the IOR, and investing Vatican capital in companies dealing with such counter-Catholic aims as arms manufacture and the production of birth control pills.

It was around this time that Sindona discovered Roberto Calvi at Banco Ambrosiano – one of several Catholic banks – and initiated him into a clandestine money-making pact, the political ramifications of which would be handled by

The Vatican was quick to close ranks when God's Banker was found dead.

none other than P2's head honcho, Licio Gelli. In accordance with the terms of the deal, Calvi established offshore accounts in fabricated corporations to move around huge sums of Vatican money, all the while skimming off the top of mafia investments in Banco Ambrosiano to fill in the holes.

The plan soon began to fall apart. In June 1982, Banco Ambrosiano was revealed to be holding debts of up to $1.5 billion, and the whole house of cards came crashing down. On 10 June, Calvi shaved his moustache, purchased a fake passport and fled to Venice, where he then hired a plane to London. On the 17th, his secretary penned an angry note condemning Calvi for the whole affair and then jumped to her death from a fifth-floor window of the Banco Ambrosiano building. The next morning, Calvi's body was discovered.

The Vatican reaction was to quickly close ranks. Following a payout of $145 million to indignant creditors, Paul Marcinkus, then head of the IOR, was brought into the Vatican and protected from investigation by sovereign immunity, which he retained until his death in 2006. He only once commented on the scandal, noting that 'you can't run the Church on Hail Marys'.

*Cardinal Paul
Marcinkus,
American-born
head of the
Vatican Bank
from 1971 to
1989. Although
implicated in
the collapse of
the Banco
Ambrosiana
scandal,
Marcinkus was
never indicted.*

An Unpleasant Echo

On 21 July 2006, a grim reminder of the Calvi affair came in the form of the dismembered body of a respected Italian banker and high-ranking Opus Dei member, found beneath a road bridge near Parma, Italy.

The victim, Gianmario Roveraro, had been leaving an Opus meeting when he disappeared on 5 July. A subsequent phone call to his wife – announcing that he was in Austria, and that everything was fine – was taken by her

The remains of banker and Opus Dei member Gianmario Roveraro, discovered beneath a motorway bridge in July 2006.

to be a coded cry for help, as he had never been to Austria but had recently set up a deal with an Austrian firm in which an Italian financial consultant, Filippo Botteri, had lost $3.2 million.

Botteri was brought in for questioning and confessed to the killing after the discovery of the remains, which were cut up with a chainsaw and half hidden in a black plastic bin liner. Botteri had initially found a means of transferring over $13 million from Roveraro's account to his own in regular instalments; when concerned bank authorities froze the account, however, Botteri panicked and murdered the banker.

Opus Dei went as far as honouring Roveraro as having 'already received from God the reward for his many virtues' – an uncharacteristic break from its usual code of silence.

Botteri was brought in for questioning and confessed to the killing after the discovery of the remains, which were cut up with a chainsaw and half hidden in a plastic bin liner.

The Swiss Guard Murders

Murders in the Vatican are usually the stuff of smoke and mirrors, but this one was painted in cold blood for all to see. Not that the resulting picture was any clearer for it.

On the night of 4 May 1998, Cedric Tornay, a lance corporal in the Swiss Guard, murdered his superior officer and his wife in their Vatican residence before turning the gun on himself. The victim, Alois Estermann, had been appointed Commander of the Swiss Guard just ten hours earlier. The motive? A fit of jealous rage. At least, that was the official line.

The speed with which the Vatican press officer, Joaquin Navarro-Valls, appeared at the gates – just hours after the bodies had been discovered – raised suspicions as to why the authorities were so keen to close the case. "The information that has emerged up to this point," he said, "allows for the theory of a fit of madness."

A smear campaign against Cedric Tornay was set in motion by the Vatican.

This was interesting, as Navarro-Valls had never met the accused. Nor had Cardinal Alfons Stickler, who that evening described Cedric Tornay as "an individual suffering from the psychological disorder of paranoia".

The autopsies, meanwhile, were carried out behind closed doors by Vatican doctors who were sworn to secrecy and kept no written records of their findings, but the news that traces of cannabis had been found in Tornay's bloodstream was immediately made public. All of which sits rather uneasily with Tornay's sterling reputation.

He had held the position of lance corporal for three years, during which time he'd been in charge of guarding the pope's own apartments in the Apostolic Palace, and was spoken of fondly by former colleagues, many of whom had been his subordinates. It wasn't enough, however, to stop a smear campaign being set in motion.

Alois Estermann in the arms room of the Vatican. To this day, the circumstances surrounding his gruesome death are a source of much controversy.

Estermann was virtually eulogized, his life and good deeds reported in detail both in the pages of *L'Osservatore Romano* and on Vatican Radio, and the requiem mass at his funeral was performed by the Cardinal Secretary of State – a rare honour for a layman. Tornay, meanwhile, was interred in the tiny church of St Anne, on the border of the Vatican. The crowd, which spilled out on to the street, contained members of the Swiss Guard.

An Issue of Motive

There are various conspiracy theories surrounding the deaths of Estermann and Tornay. One implies that the pair had been engaged in a homosexual affair, which Estermann had broken off following his promotion, and that Tornay's crime was actually one of passion.

Another, more sinister, concerns Opus Dei, which Tornay was alleged to have been investigating as a double agent on behalf of a Vatican spy ring, concerned with how far the sect had penetrated the Swiss Guard. Estermann was believed to be a devout Opus member who regularly tried to rally other officers to the cause, and some argue that it was actually he who killed Tornay, after finding out that his subordinate had been spying on him, and then turned the gun on himself and his wife – a theory that might account for the swiftness of the official line from Navarro-Valls, himself a high-ranking Opus member.

Finally, there is the theory espoused in John Follain's book *City Of Secrets*. Follain notes that Tornay was one of a minority of French-speaking Swiss Guards, who were regularly subject to continual abuse from the majority German-speaking contingent – and none of them was worse than Estermann himself. When the issue of Tornay's promotion to lance corporal was raised, Estermann was the only officer to formally oppose it (he was overruled), and later he used his superiority over the young French speaker to engage in an endless campaign of humiliation and intimidation.

Tornay stuck it out, most likely because he was determined to receive the Benemerenti Medal, awarded to all Swiss Guards after three years of service. When the medal list was finally posted, however, Tornay found his name had been withheld by Estermann for no reason other than to torment him. Tornay snapped, wrote a last letter to his mother and headed out to find Estermann, a loaded gun at his side.

Tornay is alleged to have been investigating Opus Dei on behalf of a Vatican spy ring.

In the Name of the Mother

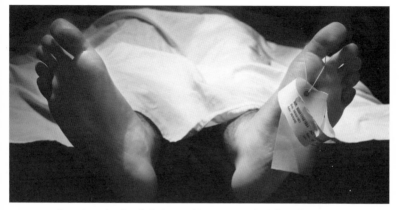

Tornay's mother literally had to steal her own son's body from the morgue

Among those people convinced of a cover-up is Muguette Baudat, Tornay's mother. When Mme Baudat wrote to the pope to challenge the story of her son's death, a Vatican official travelled to her home and she says made threats about her children.

Such threats though have not dissuaded her. When her son's body was flown home, she literally stole it from a Swiss morgue and commissioned a second autopsy, the results of which are shocking. The exit wound in his skull was 7mm in diameter, despite the fact that Tornay's service revolver used 9mm bullets; his front teeth were broken off, as if the gun had been forced into his mouth before being fired; and his lungs contained blood and saliva, most likely the result of powerful blows to the head before he died.

Horrified by the findings, Baudat has hired lawyers and presented the Vatican with a report disputing the official line and calling for an independent investigation. As these lawyers are not accredited by the papacy, however, the Vatican has not responded.

Tornay's Last Letter

Perhaps the most controversial
piece of evidence in the Swiss
Guard murder case is Cedric
Tornay's 'last letter' to his
mother, which has been deemed
a forgery by professional
graphologists and psychologists
alike. It's not hard to see why:

■ Tornay refers to his sister as
'Melinda', despite having always
called her by her nickname,
'Dada'.

■ Tornay mentions the pope by
name, despite having always
referred to him as 'the Holy
Father'.

■ The letter is addressed to
Mme Chamorel, although every
one of his previous letters was
addressed to Mme Baudat, his
mother's maiden name. Chamorel,
however, is the name that appears
on the Vatican registers.

■ There is a sinister discrepancy in dates.
Tornay mentions having been in service for
'three years, six months and six days',

Tornay's last letter is a Pandora's Box of contradictory evidence.

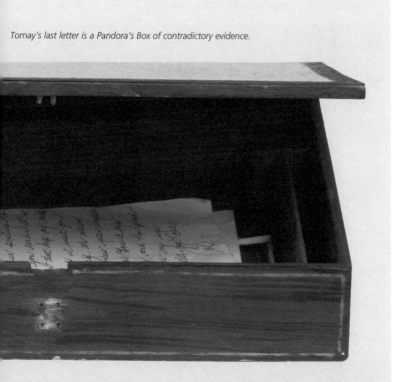

despite having been in the Swiss Guard for only three years, five months and three days at the time of his death. This has led some to believe that an assassination had been planned for a later date (7 June) but then pushed forward at the last minute.

PART FIVE
The Hidden Vatican

This final section deals with exactly that: those chapters of Vatican
history that have remained hidden from the public eye, existing largely
in rumours, fragments and decaying remains.

*The four cloaked officials
of the Vatican Secret
Archives stand guard at
the Tower of Winds.*

As a testament to the power of the
Vatican when it comes to concealing
incriminating evidence, we begin with a
look at the Vatican Secret Archives, the
Church's notoriously inaccessible
repository for all manner of records.
Following this, we outline the papacy's
culpability in one of the most bloody-
minded and brutal episodes of all time:
the Crusades.

The failure of the Crusades led to the
terrible reign of the Inquisition, which is
examined here, before we move onto the
shady world of exorcism. This is followed
by an examination of the Vatican's
affiliations with the Nazi Party under Pope
Pius XII. We then turn to the unsettling
role in the Vatican of the devout religious
sect Opus Dei, the exponentially
increasing power of which has led to
concerned insiders half-jokingly referring
to the many tentacles of the 'Oct-Opus'.

Lastly, we investigate conjecture that the
bloodline of Christ was passed on through
a child born of Mary Magdalene – a
theory that has recently captured the
public imagination through Dan Brown's
recent bestseller *The Da Vinci Code*.

The Vatican Secret Archives

With millions of documents stored across more than 50km of shelving, it's little wonder that the Archivio Segreto Vaticano attracts the attention it does. For many, however, it's the 'Segreto' part of the equation that makes the Vatican's literary vaults so intriguing.

Off limits to all but the most persistent of scholars, access to the Secret Archives is granted only by a lengthy application procedure, in which academics must not only prove their need for access, but also specifically request the items they wish to study. This is problematic, considering the enormous gaps that exist in the index catalogue – for starters, all archived material pre-dating the 8th century has mysteriously disappeared, in the Vatican's own words, 'for reasons not entirely known'. So the question remains: what exactly does the Church have in there that it's so keen on keeping to itself?

According to the authorities, the archive in its earliest incarnation contained only official documents pertaining to the Church's most wealthy patrons, but it is widely believed to have also been used as a repository for heretical works, the collection of which would slowly grow to take in the libraries of groups like the Cathars and the Knights Templar (the latter holding fast to the connection between Christ's bloodline and the Frankish Merovingian dynasty that inspired Dan Brown's *The Da Vinci Code*), and leading to the publication of an official Vatican Index of Prohibited Books in 1557.

The irony of keeping such works was that heresy hunters of the Church inevitably read them in an effort to know their enemies better, but often ended up dabbling in dark arts themselves – a dichotomy explored in Umberto Eco's novel *The Name Of The Rose.*

Just what is contained in the Secret Archives that the Church wants to hide so badly?

A letter
handwritten by
the artist
Michelangelo,
one of countless
cultural
treasures in the
vaults of the
Secret Archives.

Highlights from the Archives

1246

A letter from the Mongolian ruler Great Khan Güyük to Pope Innocent IV, rejecting the pope's claim that the Great Khan needs to be baptized and refusing to enter into peaceful relations with the Church until the pope himself goes to pay homage at the Mongolian Court.

1318

A document signalling the foundation of the University of Cambridge by Pope John XXII.

1534

A petition on behalf of the English King Henry VIII seeking papal annulment of his 24-year marriage to Catherine of Aragon so that he might marry Anne Boleyn. The reams of red ribbon attached to the bottom – the seals of 85 English noblemen attempting to convince the pope of the legitimacy of Henry's case – are said to be the origin of the term 'red tape'.

1535

A letter from Pope Paul III to the artist Michelangelo, to whom he refers in the opening paragraph as 'the glory of our century', asking the artist to continue his work on the Sistine Chapel ceiling, originally commissioned by Paul's predecessor, Clement VII.

1550

One of the last remaining letters by Michelangelo himself, pleading the case of the guards of St Peter's Basilica, whom he says have not been paid in three months and may desert their posts unless remuneration is forthcoming. Iron in the ink used to write the letter has turned corrosive, leaving the paper full of tiny slashes.

1633

Handwritten records of the Inquisition's trial of Galileo for his heretical claims that the earth revolved around the sun.

1770

Award of the Papal Equestrian Order of the Golden Spur granted to Mozart for his musical achievements.

1797

Peace treaty between the Holy See and Napoleon's French Republic, signed by the young dictator himself.

*Henry VIII embraced Catholicism – Cardinal Wolsey, pictured, was a close ally – until
the pope's refusal to annul the marriage between the king and Catherine of Aragon.*

Reading Between the Lines

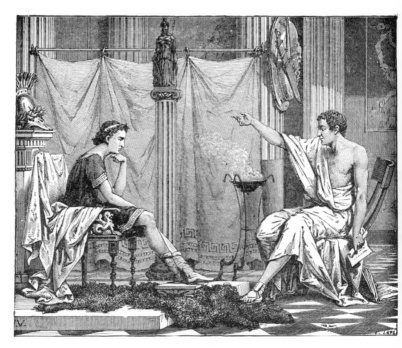

The philosopher Aristotle, here tutoring a young Alexander the Great, is believed to have penned a second book of Poetics – on comedy – *that is rumoured to be in the Secret Archives.*

Certain documents we know are gathering dust in the Secret Archives; it's those we can only guess at, however, that generate the most excitement. The following comprises a handful of potential highlights from writings rumoured to be lurking in the Vatican vaults.

■ The legendary lost second book of Aristotle's *Poetics* – on comedy – a fictionalized version of which appears at

the heart of Umberto Eco's monastic murder mystery *The Name Of The Rose*.

■ Countless apocryphal Christian writings – many of them gospels penned by contemporaries of Jesus himself – that were left out of the 'official' Old and New Testaments of the Bible as codified by Pope Damasus I in 382 AD.

■ The original text of Pope Urban II's speech from the Council of Clermont, in 1095, which inspired tens of thousands of ill-prepared Crusaders to pick up arms and head for the Holy Land.

■ The libraries of the heretical Frankish Cathars, which may well contain documents referring to the alleged union of Jesus and Mary Magdalene – a secret some say the group was eliminated for trying to protect.

■ Evidence pertaining to torture methods unofficially sanctioned by the Vatican for use by the Papal and Spanish Inquisitions, including the application of a gruesome head vice and a drawn out means of mechanical disembowelling.

■ Heretical Gnostic writings, including texts by groups such as the Orphites –

who worshipped Lucifer as the 'Light Bringer' and the serpent as the giver of knowledge – and the Borborites, who are rumoured to have feasted on aborted foetuses and to have drunk human blood.

■ Buried evidence of dark dealings by Vatican authorities since the birth of Christianity; from sacrificial murder and devil worship to the more recent controversy surrounding paedophile priests.

■ The real Third Secret of Fatima: the released version – a long-winded religious allegory – is far less incendiary than the papacy first implied, leading many to believe that the actual prophecy remains under lock and key in the archives.

■ The official autopsy report on the short-lived Pope John Paul I, possibly the only document able to confirm the popular theory that his death, just 33 days after taking office, was the result of digitalis poisoning.

■ Detailed reports of various Vatican exorcisms throughout the ages – including one believed to have been performed by Pope John Paul II in 1982.

A History of the Archives

Even the most obsessive hoarders have nothing on the popes, who have been hanging on to every scrap of paper – from personal letters to formal papal documents – since time immemorial. The vast bulk of this material was simply passed on from pope to pope until 649 AD, when the collection found its first official home in the vaults of the Lateran Palace of Rome. In the 11th century, the archives were moved to a holding place on the slopes of Palatine Hill, by which point many of the oldest papyri were already disintegrating.

These days, Palatine Hill is little more than a cluster of ruins and half-collapsed towers, but it was once home to the original Vatican archives.

During the Middle Ages, the archives were significantly devalued by being moved around a great deal, in 1245 ferried to a monastery in Cluny, and thence to Perugia, Assisi and finally Avignon, where they remained for more than a century. It wasn't until the rule of Pope Martin V (1427-1431) that the monumental process of moving the archives back to Rome began, by boat and wagon – the tribulations of which led to a great number of official documents being lost or ruined.

Napoleon's attempt to move the entire archives to France took three years, with countless documents lost along the way.

(1198-1216), who devised the Vatican Registers to keep copies of the most important papal letters, but it was Nicholas V (1447-1455) who officially founded the Vatican Library, and Sixtus V (1585-1590) who organized the Secret Archives into eighty separate cabinets or 'amaria' (which are still in existence to this very day).

And yet, despite this, the collection still had one last journey to undertake – and it was arguably the most destructive in its history. After his invasion of Rome at the turn of the 19th century, Napoleon decided to transport the entire Vatican Library to France, a task involving the shipment of 3,239 separate chests, which took three whole years to complete. Following his defeat in 1814, the archives began their slow return home, although so many carts plunged into rivers and rattled off cliffs en route that only 2,200 made it all the way back to Rome.

By this point, it was obvious that some formal system was needed to prevent further dissolution of the Church's literary heritage. The first attempt at cataloguing the collection had come during the reign of Pope Innocent II

Lost for Words: A Problem of Access

Leo XIII was the first pope to open the Vatican Secret Archives to the public – or, at least, parts of it: much of the collection remains off limits to this day.

In 2005, a Jewish group threatened to sue the Vatican for refusing to allow them access to restricted wartime documents, which they believed would identify Jewish children baptized as Catholics and separated from their families for their protection in the Second World War.

The Vatican's problem was not with the claim itself, but with its timing. When the Secret Archives were first opened to the public by Pope Leo XIII on 1 January 1881, only those records covering the reign of Paul V (1605-1621) were made available; from that point on, sections of the archives were opened sequentially, not simultaneously, with any given pope preparing that portion of materials pertaining to a pontiff that preceded him.

In early 2006, for example, Pope Benedict XVI made available those records covering the reign of Pius XI (1922-1939); the wartime documents in question, however, cover the pontificate of his successor, Pius XII, and won't be available for some time yet.

The Prefect of the Secret Archives, Father Sergio Pagano, seemed unsympathetic to the Jewish claim, noting that when "documents can be consulted, those who seemed interested don't turn up, or come for what is basically a tourist visit."

He expressed surprise that only a trickle of academics had visited a recent exhibition relating to the Vatican's efforts to help POWs in the Second World War – but then, the Church has no need to hide information like that...

The Prefect of the Secret Archives seemed unsympathetic to the Jewish claim.

The Church and the Crusades

As with all great speeches, Pope Urban II's rallying call at the 1095 Grand Council of Clermont tapped into a sense of widespread indignation and united people in a call to action; unlike many, it led directly to one of the most regrettable episodes in world history.

Pope Urban II's call to arms was more effective than anyone could have predicted.

The lead-up to Clermont dates back to 638 AD, when Jerusalem was overrun by Muslim Saracens headed by Caliph Omar, a close companion of the Prophet Mohammad; it wasn't until 1009, however, when Caliph Al Hakim bi Amr Allah laid siege to the Church of the Holy Sepulchre – built on the spot where Jesus is believed to have been crucified and then buried – that the Church began contemplating revenge.

The foundations of the Crusades were laid by Pope Gregory VII, whose victory over the Holy Roman Emperor in 1076 effectively granted the Church control over a vast military force should it ever decide to embark upon a holy war; when the Byzantine Emperor Alexius I began calling for help against marauding Seljuk Turks in 1095, Pope Urban II decided to do just that.

"This royal city," he declared, "situated at the centre of the earth, is now held captive by the enemies of Christ and is subjected, by those who do not know God, to the worship of the heathen…

Accordingly, undertake this journey eagerly for the remission of your sins, with the assurance of the reward of imperishable glory in the Kingdom of Heaven."

After hearing the bold claim that simple participation in the Crusades would guarantee warriors an automatic pardon from all worldly sins and assure them a place in Heaven, the crowds are reported to have responded with impassioned cries of "Deus vult" ("God wills it").

Word spread and a force slowly amassed, composed of as many peasants as professional knights – even monks and women found their way into the charge. The world was about to pay for Urban II's religious conviction.

Urban's call to arms was taken up eagerly in the West, and the Crusade was quickly set in motion.

The Hapless Hermit

The first wave of holy warriors wasn't an official crusader force per se, but rather a motley rabble of disorganized and largely unarmed peasants led by a priest of Amiens called Peter the Hermit, who had himself undertaken a pilgrimage to Jerusalem several years previously but been captured en route, tortured by Turks and forced to turn back.

His 'People's Crusade', as it came to be known, departed in April 1096 and arrived in Constantinople three months later. Their appearance was far from welcome: loathe to sustain an army of peasants – especially with the real crusaders just weeks away – Alexius urged Peter's force to cross the Bosporus and await further orders.

Instead, the eager paupers ill-advisedly entered Turkish territory, where they were slaughtered in their thousands by an overwhelming Seljuk army. By the time the retreating shreds of the People's Crusade had made it safely back to the walls of Constantinople, up to 20,000 are believed to have been killed.

Around the same time, a second force

of roughly 10,000 German crusaders left Cologne and headed northwards up the Rhine Valley (in the opposite direction to Jerusalem), arbitrarily pillaging, torturing and executing as they went. The brunt of their brutal zeal fell upon the European Jews, who

Peter the Hermit travelled the length and breadth of Europe rallying peasants to join his unofficial 'People's Crusade', which ended in ignominy and bloody defeat.

were considered responsible for the crucifixion of Christ, and who were anyway much closer and easier to kill than Muslims in a far-off land.

As news of the horrific slaughter spread quickly up the Rhine Valley, many Jews committed suicide en masse to save themselves from having to choose between death at the hands of the crusaders or forced conversion, and the German Crusade actually became written into history as the very first example of an anti-Semitic pogrom.

Thy Will be Done?

The real First Crusade arrived in Constantinople in December 1096, mere months after the abortive People's Crusade. Also known as the Princes' or Barons' Crusade, this was a more formidable force of trained warriors, and they quickly recaptured Byzantium (although Emperor Alexius, afraid that the over-enthusiastic crusaders would sack the key city of Nicea, secretly accepted its surrender).

After regaining their strength – and amalgamating into their army the remnants of the People's Crusade, including Peter the Hermit himself – the fighters began the long and highly unpleasant march to Jerusalem. One knight, Stephen of Blois, wrote in a letter of the generally held belief that the journey would take them five weeks; in fact, it went on for more than two years, with many men and horses lost to a combination of hunger, heat and illness, and even some resorting to cannibalism to survive.

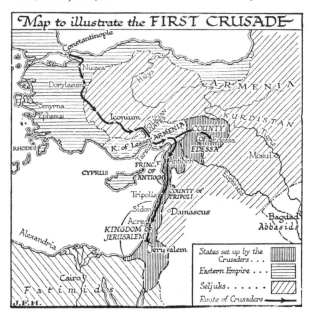

A map showing the route taken by the warriors of the First Crusade in their two-year trek from Constantinople to the walls of Jerusalem.

When they finally reached Jerusalem, on 7th May 1099, the crusaders instigated one of the most terrible massacres in history, surmounting its defensive walls with siege towers built from dismantled ships and then rampaging through the city, reputedly singing hymns as they slaughtered every man, woman and child regardless of their religion (many Jews and Eastern Christians were slain alongside the Muslims).

After storming the defensive walls of Jerusalem, the crusaders rampaged the city, killing virtually everything that moved.

The stories that accompany the siege – of crusaders wading through ankle-deep rivers of blood and disembowelling bodies to find swallowed gold – are like apocalyptic parables from the Book of Revelations. And yet, despite severe losses within the Princes' Crusade (of roughly 7,000 that set out, only 1,500 are believed to have made it as far as the walls of Jerusalem, let alone survived the siege), the dramatic recapture of the holy city ensured that the First Crusade was written into history as a stunning victory, and set the tone for more than a century of crusades to come.

Heretics at Home

The apparent success of the First Crusade led to a profound belief that it had revealed the best way to establish a Christian world, and the following century saw no fewer than eight subsequent crusades (not to mention the largely fictionalized Children's Crusade – see picture), which only increased in frequency following the recapture of Jerusalem by Saladin, Sultan of Egypt, in 1187. And yet, despite occasional victories (the taking of the Egyptian city of Damietta during the Fifth Crusade of 1219, for example), none replicated the initial zeal of the first, and before long they had become little more than exercises in secular expansion by the crowned heads of Europe.

By the early 13th century, with the impotence of far-flung crusades painfully exposed, the Church turned its wrath on heretics closer to home, instigating the Albigensian Crusade to flush the sectarian Cathar community out of southern France.

On 22 July 1209, the entire population of Bezier was slaughtered – up to 20,000 men, women and children – despite the coastal town containing no more than 500 Cathars. When asked by one concerned crusader how they would know their enemies from ordinary French citizens, the papal legate Arnaud-Amaury is said to have responded: "Kill them all, for the Lord knows which are his own."

On 22 July 1209, the entire population of Bezier was slaughtered – up to 20,000 men, women and children – despite the coastal town containing no more than 500 Cathars.

Much myth-making surrounds the enigmatic Children's Crusade. Some say that it began when a boy was visited by Jesus, who told him to take up arms against the enemy and advance on the Holy Land. Legend then has it that this same boy managed to amass an army of no less than 20,000 on his journey towards the Mediterranean. The crusade ended in disaster, however, with the majority of children either dying before they reached the sea, or being picked up by boats upon their arrival and sold into slavery on foreign shores.

In Good Faith: The Inquisitions

The Vatican's current Congregation for the Doctrine of the Faith didn't always have such an innocuous name: when it was first established in 1542, it was known as the Supreme Sacred Congregation of the Roman and Universal Inquisition – and it struck fear into the hearts of millions.

The Inquisition itself, however, can be traced back even further – to the Albigensian Crusade's ruthless elimination of French Cathars between 1209 and 1229, which initiated a new kind of holy war and set the stage for one of the most shameful acts in Vatican history.

In 1215, Pope Innocent III convened the Fourth Lateran Council, which ordered Jews and Muslims to wear badges distinguishing them from Christians and codified Church policy against heretics – including the notion that anyone shielding a heretic should receive the same punishment as the heretic himself, or that unrepentant and relapsed heretics should be given steeper sentences, including the confiscation of family property by the Church or even death.

This ideology was based largely on the merciless 'fire and brimstone' outlook of the Old Testament. The Book of Deuteronomy, for example, notes that, if the people of a town are being led astray by false gods, 'you must certainly put to the sword all who live in that town. Destroy it completely, both its people and its livestock'. When the Inquisition was officially founded by Pope Gregory IX in 1232, such ideas helped form the blueprint for its brutal persecution.

Jews and Muslims were forced to wear badges to distinguish them from Christians.

*The Vatican's war on 'false Christians' was as relentless
as it was barbaric, as evidenced by this 1893 painting.*

The Papal Inquisition

The age of the Papal Inquisition was quite possibly the Vatican's darkest hour.

At the centre of all religous trials was a Chief Inquisitor. It was his job to travel from parish to parish preaching against heresy and nailing up 'Edicts of Faith', which would allow local townspeople to recognize signs of heresy among them.

There then followed a one- to four-week 'Term of Grace', in which confessions of heresy were voluntary and rewarded with limited punishments. After this, anyone who had not yet confessed was in danger of being denounced by others, with disgruntled employees regularly accusing their bosses, husbands and wives able to accuse each other and even the word of convicted criminals (and heretics) taken under oath.

The resulting atmosphere was one of extreme paranoia. Evidence from only two witnesses was needed for a successful prosecution, and the accused were never told the names of their accusers.

Those willing to confess early on were let off with more lenient punishments (fines, for example, or religious pilgrimages), while those who relapsed or refused to recant in the first place were given the harshest penalties, including the confiscation of property by the Church and burning at the stake – the latter seen as a theologically justifiable form of execution in that it didn't draw blood. The same was true of the Inquisition's favoured forms of torture (water torture was popular, as was roasting the feet over burning coals). Torture is now believed to have been used to extract confessions in a third of all trials held by the Inquisition.

Flogging was a popular form of torture, as was roasting the feet over burning coals.

The Spanish Inquisition

Torture was obviously carried out behind closed doors, but executions were highly social events, held in town squares and attended by enormous crowds. This was never more true that during the ceremonial 'auto de fe' (Act of Faith) of the Spanish Inquisition: in 1660, one auto de fe in Seville is recorded as lasting for three days and being attended by over 100,000 people.

Confessions were extracted by means of torture both cruel and unusual: here, a suspected heretic is strapped to a wheel and then slowly rotated over an open fire.

Indeed, the Papal Inquisition may have set new records in religious intimidation and persecution, but they were roundly smashed in almost all respects by the Spanish Inquisition, founded by King Ferdinand and Queen Isabella in 1480 as a means rooting out all false Christians – especially Jews and Muslims – from across their homeland.

Nor were these unrealistic aims: the Spanish Inquisition's most famous Chief Inquisitor, Tomás de Torquemada, succeeded in having all non-repentant Jews ejected from Spain by 1492 (50,000 accepted conversion, meaning that between 100,000 to 200,000 must

have fled), while up to three million Muslims had evacuated the country by 1615.

The Spanish Inquisition's thoroughness was exceeded only by its severity. Methods of torture were wider ranging: the rack was regularly employed, as was water torture and the dislocation of joints by lifting the body with ropes binding the wrists behind the back. Execution was similarly gruesome, with the condemned given one last chance to recant at the stake: if they did so, they were garrotted before the fires were lit; if not, they were burned alive – sometimes, if they vocally stuck to their guns, slow burning 'green wood' was used to make the process longer and more painful.

Equally appalling was the common practice of exhuming and burning the bodies of those condemned posthumously, which allowed the Church to confiscate their families' property and possessions. It all sounds like the very definition of medieval barbarity, but such practices actually went on until the Spanish Inquisition was officially disbanded in 1834. By that time it had tried roughly 150,000 people, between 3,000 and 5,000 of whom are believed to have been put to death.

A merciful release: a hapless victim is garrotted before being burnt, and thus spared the pain of the flames.

145

A World in Motion: The Galileo Affair

Galileo was twice forced to stand trial for his 'heretical' theory that the earth revolved around the sun. The second time, under the threat of execution, he recanted.

Galileo Galilei is perhaps the best known victim of the Papal Inquisition; what is less well known is that he was actually revered by the Church as a master of 'natural

philosophy' (as science was then known) before his experiments with telescopes in 1609 brought him into direct conflict with it.

The observations described in his book *The Starry Messenger* – including the discovery of spots on the sun and mountains on the moon – were certainly revolutionary, but didn't clash with the Aristotelian notions commonly held by the Catholic Church at the time. What did cause problems, however, were his later views supporting the Copernican notion of a heliocentric solar system in which the earth revolved around the sun – a huge departure from the Biblical idea that the earth was in fact at the very centre of the universe.

As a result, Galileo was called twice to recant before the Inquisition. The first time, in 1615, he did so voluntarily, but was ordered to appear again in 1633 following the publication of his *Dialogue Concerning The Two Chief World Systems*, which had actually been commissioned by the Inquisition in an attempt to present both sides of the argument, but which was deemed to have given far too much weight to the Copernican view.

At this second trial, Galileo was made to state that the idea of a fixed sun was 'absurd in philosophy and formally heretical', and that the notion of an orbital earth was 'erroneous in faith'; the offending book was also banned (as were all other works by Galileo, past and as yet unwritten), and he was sentenced to a life in prison, later commuted to house arrest at his villa in Arcetri, where he died less than ten years later. The written records of his trial remain locked in the Vatican Secret Archives to this day.

Dancing with the Devil

Those familiar with its Hollywood history may think that exorcism is mere horror movie fodder and in times gone by, a thorny subject that the Vatican has preferred not to comment on. But behind the scenes, exorcism has become big business for the Church.

So big, in fact, that the main pontifical university in Rome recently offered a two-month exorcism course. The movies aren't far off the mark in their portrayal of this ancient practice either; many Catholic priests argue that *The Exorcist* (1973), one of the most controversial films of all time, was actually accurate in its representation of an exorcism performed on a young girl.

This seems to be confirmed by the exorcist's industry handbook, the 84-page *Of Exorcisms and Certain Supplications*. Despite being updated in 1998 for the first time in almost 400 years (to emphasize the importance of considering psychological solutions before embarking on spiritual crusades, and to remove references to the 'smell' and 'colour' of the devil, who is now believed to be without form), the book reveals just how traditional a practice this is.

Firstly, the exorcist must ask God to intervene on behalf of the possessed soul (the 'imploring formula'); if nothing happens, he must then attempt to forcibly remove the demon or demons himself (the 'imperative formula'). This is done through a mixture of prayers, blessings and incantations conducted entirely in Latin, although part of the original English translation remains ("Give place, abominable creature, give way, you monster, give way to Christ...").

The priest is advised not to become distracted by demonic chatter along the way, but to focus on the task at hand. After all, the demon could be Satan himself, in which case the process is certain to be a long and arduous one.

Of the countless Catholic exorcists, one – Father Gabriele Amorth – towers above all others. As Senior Exorcist to the Vatican, he claims to have

Scene from the horror film The Exorcist – *the exorcism performed by the priest character on the young possessed girl in the movie is said to be close to the real ceremony.*

performed over 50,000 exorcisms (taking anything from a few minutes to a few days each), and is visited on a daily basis by seemingly possessed pilgrims from across the world. Amorth famously claims that both Hitler and Stalin were possessed by Satan, and insists that Pope Pius XII once attempted a long-distance exorcism on the former – unsuccessful, sadly, due to the geographical limitations of the Vatican-based ceremony.

Exorcisms through the Ages

WILLIAM PERRY, 1620

After claiming to have been cursed by an old crone, young Master Perry fell into fits so violent that it took four men to hold him down. He also vomited pins, wool and feathers, and was driven insensible by readings of the gospels. A Catholic priest was called upon to conduct an exorcism, which was unsuccessful. Later, the wily Lord Bishop of Lichfield exposed Perry as a fake by reading him passages of the gospels in Greek, which Perry failed to react to – the devil, claimed the bishop, understood all languages. As if to confirm the Lord Bishop's theory, Perry was later discovered attempting to colour his urine with black ink. He fell into a crying fit and confessed everything.

ROBBIE, 1949

The 14-year-old boy known only as 'Robbie' began displaying symptoms of a powerful possession after dabbling with a Ouija board with his aunt in their Maryland home. Scratching noises began emanating from inside the walls, objects inexplicably lurched around his room and one local priest even witnessed him levitating in his chair. Two more high-ranking priests were summoned – Fathers William Bowden and Walter Halloran – who embarked upon a long and tortuous exorcism during which the boy repeatedly vomited, babbled in Latin and displayed words and symbols in the form of supernatural cuts and rashes on his body. That same year, a young Georgetown University student named William Peter Blatty read a description of the haunting in the *Washington Post*; twenty years later, it would inspire his seminal horror novel, *The Exorcist*.

ANNALIESE MICHEL, 1976

A devout Catholic, German-born Annaliese attributed more than a decade of psychic disturbance to possession, withdrawing herself from medical treatment and applying to the Church for an exorcism, which was eventually granted. She was told that she was possessed by six demons: Lucifer, Cain, Nero, Judas, Hitler and a deranged 17th century priest. She died following one of her weekly sessions with the priests – Pastor Ernst Alt and Arnold Renz – both of whom were convicted, along with Annaliese's parents, of manslaughter. During their trial, tapes were played that the defence claimed portrayed the sounds of demons arguing during the exorcism. Annaliese's story was relocated to America for the movie *The Exorcism Of Emily Rose* (2005).

MOTHER TERESA OF CALCUTTA, 1997

While on her deathbed, the Roman Catholic nun and devout missionary Mother Teresa began suffering from troubled visions and disturbed sleep. Concerned that she was being 'harassed by Satan', the Archbishop of Calcutta, Henry D'Souza, ordered a rudimentary exorcism to be performed over her frail body. The act was seen by many as having been rash and unnecessary, although D'Souza later claimed that it was a mere 'prayer of protection', given with her consent, and not a full ritual exorcism in the traditional sense.

Even the devout Mother Teresa was rumoured to be under threat from Satan on her deathbed.

When the Devil visited the Vatican

On a September afternoon in 2000, the hushed reverence that usually accompanies papal appearances in St Peter's Square was shattered by a terrible scream.

At the edges of the assembled crowd, a 19-year-old girl from the Italian city of Monza had begun hurling obscenities at John Paul II in what onlookers described as a 'cavernous voice'. When security guards attempted to restrain her, she reportedly shook them off with superhuman strength.

The pope asked that the girl be brought to him, and – convinced that she was possessed by demonic forces – performed an impromptu exorcism in a quiet area away from the main square. It later transpired that Father Gabriele Amorth had the previous day performed an unsuccessful exorcism on this very same girl – who had been referred to him by the chief exorcist of Milan – and he did so again the day after, the pope's improvised efforts also having been unsuccessful. At this second exorcism, Amorth later reported, the demon mockingly cackled: "Not even the leader of your church can send me away!"

St Peter's Square, September 2000 – a horrific scream shatters the peace during mass.

Nor was this the first of John Paul II's exorcisms: in 1982, he locked himself away with a woman who was brought to him screaming and writhing around on the floor. Initial efforts met with strong resistance, but he finally dispelled the demon by promising to pray for the girl's soul at mass the following day.

The Vatican and the Nazis

**New evidence uncovered in the Vatican Secret Archives
suggests that the wartime Pope Pius XII – formerly an
influential Vatican diplomat named Eugenio Pacelli – may
have done more to facilitate Hitler's rise to power than
most secular leaders.**

Much of this is the result of
investigations by one man, John
Cornwell, who gained access to the
archives with the intention of
exonerating the late pontiff of such
claims, but who found himself in
such a 'state of moral shock' at
what he discovered, that his book –
Hitler's Pope – turned out very
differently indeed.

Cornwell has since distanced himself
from certain of his own arguments –
retracting some of the evil motives he
formerly ascribed to Pius and stressing
that he now finds it 'impossible to
judge' the wartime pontiff's actions;
others, meanwhile, stress that Pius
actually helped the Jews, at one point
organizing a deportation from Hungary
that saved as many as 800,000 lives. At
the same time, however, the evidence
against him is hard to simply dismiss out
of hand and is worthy of further
examination here.

The lion's share of Cornwell's work
centred on Pacelli's early years as papal
ambassador to Munich, an office he
undertook with the aim of re-
establishing the absolute power of the
Vatican in a nation that for more than
400 years had enjoyed an unusual
amount of religious autonomy. It was
here, in letters to the then Cardinal
Secretary of State dated between 1917
and 1919, that Pacelli revealed a latent
hostility to members of what he referred
to as 'the Jewish cult', describing one as
'pale, dirty, with vacant eyes, a hoarse
voice, vulgar, repulsive, with a face that
is both intelligent and sly'.

In another letter, he registered
annoyance that German Jews were
asking the Vatican to help speed up a
large delivery of palm fronds, which they
needed to celebrate the Feast of
Tabernacles, but which had been
confiscated by the Italian government.
'The Israelite community is seeking the

Eugenio Pacelli – then a Vatican diplomat, later Pope Pius XII – leaves the Berlin palace in 1929. Even then, his connection with the German powerbase was close and extremely complex.

intervention of the Pope in the hope that he will plead on behalf of a thousand German Jews,' he wrote. The irony was that soon he would be the one pleaded with, only by that time there would be six million Jews doing the pleading, and a great deal more than palm fronds at stake.

A Dictator in the Vatican

After coming to power in 1933, Hitler turned his full attention to signing the Reich Concordat with Pacelli, who was now back in the Vatican and working as Cardinal Secretary of State. The Führer's terms were calculated to nullify opposition to the Nazi Party: in exchange for being able to impose Canon Law on German Catholics, the Vatican had to persuade the German Catholic Centre Party to sign the Enabling Act, effectively disbanding one of the most significant opposition parties to the Third Reich and giving Hitler unchecked dictatorial powers.

As a result, Catholics in their millions joined the Nazi Party, believing that it had the unqualified support of the pope himself, while Hitler publicly commended the deal as "especially significant in the struggle against the international Jewry". From that point on, any German Catholic criticism of the Nazis had to be channelled through the Vatican, but the Vatican did and said nothing – very much a result of the intractable position of Pacelli himself.

In the summer of 1938, as Pope Pius XI lay dying, he became suddenly uneasy about the rise of fascism and anti-Semitism in Europe – but by then it was too late. He passed away just hours before he was due to give a speech condemning Hitler.

Pacelli, meanwhile, was elected pope after just three ballots, taking the throne as Pius XII on 12 March 1939. One of his first acts was to meet with German authorities and reaffirm his support for the Nazi Party; the following month, at Pacelli's request, the papal ambassador to Berlin hosted a gala reception to mark Hitler's 50th birthday. War was just weeks away.

Hitler knew that by disbanding the German Catholic Centre Party, he would effectively remove the final obstacle standing in the way of absolute power – and, with the Vatican's help, he succeeded.

Don't Mention the War...

Hitler invaded Poland on 1 September 1939. Much to the bafflement of the Allies, however, Pope Pius XII said nothing. He refused to condemn the Nazis even as war escalated and casualties mounted on both sides, although it was in 1942, when the world woke up to the reality of the Final Solution, that the papal silence became most unsettling.

On 16 June, the British *Daily Telegraph* ran a front page article on the extermination of the Jews; less than a week later, a massive rally in New York's Madison Square Gardens demanded world intervention in the crisis; in September, President Roosevelt sent his personal representative to the Vatican in the hope of forcing a reaction, but still the pope remained stony faced.

It was only in his Christmas message of that year, a week after the British envoy to the Vatican had personally handed him a dossier documenting the extermination of millions of Jews in concentration camps across Europe, that Pius finally spoke – but what he said was so diluted that he may as well have maintained his silence. There was no mention of 'Nazis' or 'Jews' by name, only an obscure reference to the 'hundreds of thousands' (not millions) marked for death 'by reason of their nationality or race'.

If such vague condemnation marked a shift in policy towards the Nazis, then it wasn't significant enough to save the thousand Jews rounded up from the streets of Rome by SS soldiers, right under the pope's nose, less than a year later. Of those deported, almost all were killed. One, Settimia Spizzichino, was found barely breathing in a heap of mangled corpses; she had been experimented on by the Nazi 'Angel of Death', Dr Josef Mengele.

In 1995, in an interview with the BBC, Spizzichino vented an anger felt by a great proportion of the Jewish community. "Pius XII could have warned us what was going to happen," she said, "but he was an anti-Semitic pope, a pro-

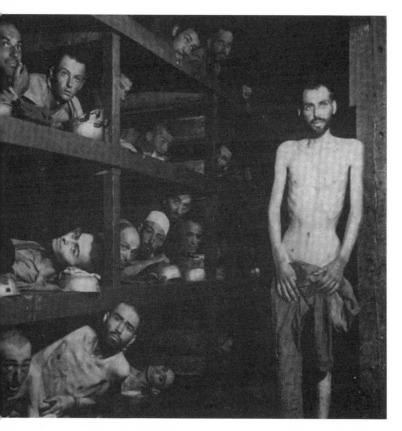

German pope. He didn't take a single
risk. And when they say that the Pope is
like Jesus Christ, it isn't true. He did not
save a single child."

*A handful of newly liberated
survivors of the Nazi death camp
at Auschwitz. Critics condemn the
Vatican's refusal to acknowledge
the full scale of the horror.*

Opening Old Wounds

Vatican affiliations with the Nazis didn't die with Pius XII. When the German Cardinal Joseph Ratzinger became Pope Benedict XVI in 2005, critics pointed to his term of service in the Hitler Youth following his 14th birthday in 1941. Membership was mandatory at the time, and his biographer insists that he undertook it unenthusiastically; it is also known that Benedict was conscripted into the German army, but deserted in May 1945. And yet, some still saw his background as inappropriate for the leader of the Catholic Church, especially in the light of the scandal surrounding Pius XII.

Things came to a head less than a year later, during a papal visit to the concentration camp at Auschwitz. Far from appearing contrite or apologizing for the part of ordinary German people in the Holocaust, Benedict further

inflamed Jewish anger by passing the blame on to a 'ring of criminals', which he said had managed to hijack the entire nation – thus implying that he and his own family were as much victims of the Nazis as the Jews themselves. Even worse, he implied that Jews were actually incidental victims in what had been, on a deeper level, an attempt by the Nazis to 'tear up the taproot of the Christian faith'.

As a result, barely half a century on from the Holocaust itself, the Vatican's murky role in one of the greatest human atrocities of the 20th century is once again under scrutiny.

Pope Benedict XVI on his controversial 2006 trip to Auschwitz. His perceived shifting of German blame caused outrage among Jewish commentators.

The Vatican and Opus Dei

Despite seeming impenetrable to outsiders, the Vatican appears to be in the grip of a force more powerful than any of its enemies. They look, speak and pray like regular Catholics, but the members of Opus Dei are changing the face of the Church as we know it.

Among the many statues that line the walls of St Peter's Basilica, the monument to St Josemaria Escriva de Balaguer looks strangely out of place, pearly white against the ash coloured rock of the alcove in which it sits and almost completely unblemished by the passing of time. Indeed, when John Paul II canonized the founder of Opus Dei in 2002, not even 30 years after his death, it caused one Cambridge historian to deem it 'the most striking example in modern times of the successful promotion of a cause by a pressure group'.

It wasn't until the following year, however, that Dan Brown's *The Da Vinci Code* gave the wider world an inkling of Escriva's 'deeply devout Catholic sect'.

The 'Fact' prefacing the book draws attention to reports of 'brainwashing, coercion and a dangerous practice known as corporeal mortification', while noting Opus' recent construction of a stunning $47 million National Headquarters on New York's Lexington Avenue. It's a million miles away from the humble society established in Madrid by Escriva, then a simple priest, in 1928. Opus Dei (literally 'Work of God') claims to help faithful Catholics around the world realize their potential as everyday saints by working hard.

Why, then, does Dan Brown choose a homicidal albino monk to portray Opus Dei as a cult bent on fear and destruction? What power does this controversial group hold both in and out of the Vatican? In the current climate of scandal and secrecy, it can be hard to separate fact from fiction.

The cilice – a self-mutilating barbed chain – is worn around the upper thigh by devout Opus Dei members almost every day of the year.

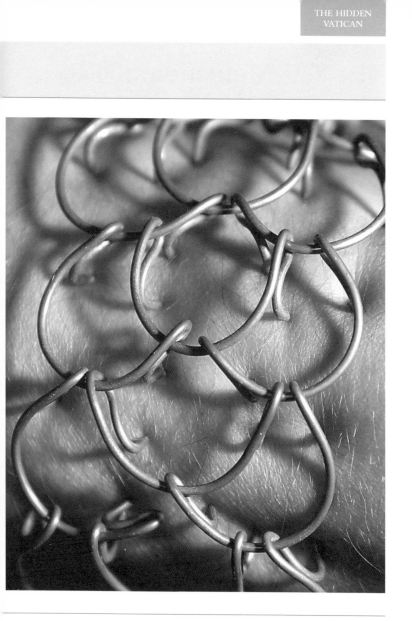

The Self-Mutilation Society

It now claims over 85,000 members worldwide, but Opus Dei was initially founded in an attempt to extend the religiosity of ordinary Spaniards beyond Sunday and into the working week, thus sanctifying the secular world.

By 1946, however, Opus Dei had extended its mission to Italy, Portugal and Britain; by 1982, the group had consolidated its power so successfully that Pope John Paul II established it as a personal prelature of the Vatican, effectively granting it the status of a 'church within the Church', and sparking rumours about the undue influence it wielded over the papacy. When Escriva was fast-tracked to sainthood in 2002, those rumours seemed to have been unofficially confirmed.

And yet, it is the more obscure Opus practices that provide the most cause for speculation – especially thanks to the surrounding veil of secrecy. What little we know is enough to set tongues wagging: the 'Heroic Minute' that follows waking, for example, in which members are encouraged to leap out of bed, kiss the floor and declare 'serviam' ('I will serve').

Then, of course, there is the small matter of corporeal mortification, which takes many forms. At one end of the scale is the simple act of sleeping on the floor, taking a cold shower or denying oneself dessert at dinner; at the other are tools for self-inflicted suffering like the 'discipline', a short whip that members apply to the back or buttocks once a week (Escriva himself was apparently so zealous in its application that he regularly splattered his bathroom walls with blood). Also popular is the 'cilice', a spiked chain worn around the upper thigh for two hours each day, leaving small holes in the flesh.

This may sound like the very definition of occult behaviour, but it comes straight from the writings of Escriva himself, who laid out his beliefs in his seminal Opus handbook, *The Way*. 'Blessed be pain,' writes Escriva, 'Loved be pain. Sanctified be pain… glorified be pain.'

The tomb of Josemaria Escriva de Balaguer, founder of Opus Dei, in the Vatican. Escriva was fast-tracked to sainthood in 2002.

The Oldest Tricks in the Book

In 1981, following a shocking expose of internal Opus practices in a British newspaper, Cardinal Basil Hume, then Archbishop of Westminster, banned the sect from recruiting under-18s in the UK.

This was a reaction to revelations about Opus recruitment methods, which remain secretive and aggressive in the extreme: in its early years, converts were encouraged not to tell family members or friends of their new lives – many were forbidden from using the phone or contacting their families.

Similarly unsettling is the way in which recruitment is tailored to target individuals: for example, if a potential recruit has a passion for skiing, Opus members may actually plan a ski trip on which to pop the big question. Nor does the pressure lie entirely on the recruits: established members are encouraged to have between 12 and 15 friends at any given time, with written profiles of each and regular reports handed to the authorities on how close they are to joining – all unbeknown to the friends themselves, obviously. Young idealists are the main targets, with the result that male Opus members are actually allowed to smoke and enter bars, so long as it is for the purpose of drawing in

potential converts. Once membership has been confirmed, however, idealism is reduced to merely following the rules to the best of one's abilities.

Many critics of Opus draw attention to the fascistic elements of Escriva's outlook as espoused in *The Way*, which states: 'You shall not buy books without the advice of an experienced Christian.' Sure enough, Opus members must ask permission from their spiritual directors before reading any book (even if it is required for a university course), while Joseph Gonzales, a former Opus 'numerary', recalled seeing the authorities regularly burning books in the garden of his centre.

A numerary, incidentally, is a Opus member that lives a celibate existence in a gender-separated Opus centre, and devotes the bulk of their income to the sect – and with 20,000 numeraries, business is booming.

Opus recruitment methods remain secretive and aggressive in the extreme.

Tammy DiNicola, a former Opus Dei member, works her way through a two-inch thick list of literature prohibited by the sect. Along with her mother (pictured left), Tammy runs the Opus Dei Awareness Network (ODAN), which offers support and information to people who have found themselves adversely affected by the organization.

Controversial Opus Members

Navarro-Valls was a hugely powerful figure within the Vatican – and in Opus Dei.

Javier Echevarria Rodriguez

The current Bishop Prelate of Opus Dei caused a huge outcry in 1997, when he asserted that 90% of disabled children, according to 'scientific research', were born to couples who had 'not entered into marriage in a pure state', and were thus paying for the sinfulness of their parents.

Joaquin Navarro-Valls

As head of the Vatican Press Office (1984-2006), Navarro-Valls made it very hard for independent investigators to assess how far Opus had penetrated the papacy – and this was never more clear than during his swift closure of the Swiss Guard murder case of 1998, which some believe may have had links to Opus Dei (see page 120).

The grip of Opus Dei extends all the way into the British government thanks to MP Ruth Kelly, who has been frank about her membership of the sect (although she's refused to confirm whether or not she wears a cilice to work).

Ruth Kelly

Kelly must have had a hard time reconciling the demands of her work as the British government's Minister for Women and Equality with the prejudices of Opus Dei (which strongly opposes homosexuality and only recently allowed its female members to wear trousers). In 2006, a UK newspaper noted that she had not supported a single piece of gay rights legislation since the Labour government came to power in 1997.

Robert Philip Hanssen

A former member of the FBI arrested in 2001 for selling US secrets to Moscow in exchange for $1.4 million in cash and diamonds, Hanssen allegedly confessed to an Opus priest early in his career, but this happened in strict confidence, and so the spying went on unchecked for several years.

The Blood of Christ

No issue blurs the boundary between fact and fiction like the alleged cover-up surrounding Christ's supposed marriage to Mary Magdalene and the perpetuation of his bloodline among Frankish kings. Most are now familiar with the story – but is that all it is?

Author Dan Brown's assertions concerning Opus Dei aren't the only 'facts' in the blockbuster book *The Da Vinci Code* to cause widespread controversy. Similarly problematic is his claim, on the opening page, that 'The Priory of Sion – a European secret society founded in 1099 – is a real organization', and that its erstwhile

members have included such cultural giants as Sir Isaac Newton, Victor Hugo and Leonardo da Vinci himself.

The credibility of a historical Priory of Sion has been almost universally debunked (see page 176), but the great secret that it is alleged to have sworn to protect continues to tantalize

on the border between fact and fiction. That secret, of course, is the alleged marriage between Jesus Christ and Mary Magdalene, a union which is said to have resulted in a child, Sarah, and later have helped found the Merovingian Dynasty of Frankish kings. The Holy Grail was long believed to have been the chalice used by Christ at the Last Supper, which later held his blood, but in this version of events it is Mary herself who is the real grail, serving as she did as the vessel for Christ's bloodline.

All of this was alleged to have been discovered in 1099 by soldiers of the First Crusade in Jerusalem, who uncovered not only Mary's venerated remains, but also documents pertaining to the marriage. Groups like the Knights Templar and the deeply spiritual Cathars subsequently took an oath to protect this secret – an oath that some say led to their being targeted by the Church both in later Crusades and by the Inquisition. This was one story that the Vatican clearly wanted to keep to itself.

History has thrown up countless artists' impressions of the Holy Grail. In recent years, however, a theory has emerged that the Grail may in fact have been a human being: Mary Magdalene.

The 'Real' Mary Magdalene

The Church's determination to repress the story of Jesus and Mary's union is rooted in an ancient fear of what is termed the 'sacred feminine' – the notion of inherently pagan female deities – and it was a fear potent enough to lead to what many claim is a Biblical cover-up of mind-blowing proportions.

The conventional figure of Mary Magdalene is that of a reformed prostitute, but conspiracy theorists maintain that this was merely part of a Catholic smear campaign used to undermine her true power. The 3rd century Gnostic Gospels, for example, discovered sealed in an earthenware vessel in 1945 by two Egyptian brothers digging for fertilizer, paint a very different portrait of Mary; one in which she is not only a morally upstanding woman of royal descent, but also closer to Jesus even than the Apostles themselves.

In one Gnostic parable, Jesus chooses Mary to relate a vision to the rest of his disciples, at which point Peter is seized by a fit of jealous rage, calming down only at the insistence of his companion, Levi. "If the Saviour made her worthy," says Levi, "who are you to reject her? Surely, the Saviour knows her very well. That is why he loved her more than us."

In 1995, Pope John Paul II used the fact that Jesus had chosen only male disciples as proof of the inherent blasphemy of ordaining female priests – an assertion that crumbles in the light of the Gnostic texts. Indeed, it was possibly to prevent the circulation of writings such as these that Pope Damasus I formally codified the Old and New Testaments of the Bible in 382 AD.

In 591 AD, when Pope Gregory I asserted that Mary Magdalene was none other than the whore saved by Jesus, he claimed simply to be clearing up confusion regarding the number of women named Mary in the Bible. In fact, he may have been deliberately attempting to erase all traces of the most powerful woman in Christian history – not only Jesus' closest confident, but possibly also his beloved wife.

> *"If the Saviour made her worthy, who are you to reject her?"*

A woman scorned: was Mary Magdalene closer to Christ than the Vatican would have us believe?

Secrets of The Last Supper

The depiction of The Last Supper *is a feast of intrigue for hungry conspiracy hunters.*

Dan Brown's claim that the story of Jesus and Mary Magdalene's marriage became the sworn secret of the ancient Priory of Sion is almost universally refuted, but the notion that Leonardo da Vinci left clues pertaining to the legend in one of his most famous works is less easy to dismiss. The painter may not have been a member of Brown's fictionalized secret society, but his 29ft-wide version of *The Last Supper* – painted on the wall of a Milanese convent between 1495 and 1498 – contains several intriguing aspects that it is possible to read as hints towards this most holy of matrimonies.

The potentially threatening gesture made by St Peter at the throat of the figure taken to be Mary is said to be a reference to his jealousy at her closeness to Christ; the absence of a chalice at the table, meanwhile, may be a sign that da Vinci was well aware that Mary was the real Holy Grail all along. Interestingly, the phantom image of a grail does appear in the wall when the viewer looks directly at the figure of St Bartholomew (at the far left of the congregation), although it is impossible to say whether this is deliberate or a mere spatial fluke.

At the centre of this theory is the belief that the figure to the viewer's left of Jesus is not the Apostle John, as initially believed, but rather Mary Magdalene herself. The form is certainly feminine – from the soft facial features and flowing hair to the hint of a bust beneath the robes – as is the slightly swooning aspect, leaning into the Apostle Peter with gentle, downcast eyes.

Then there is the strangely forced 'M' shape formed by the diverging figures of Jesus, St Peter and the one believed to be Mary – a possible hint at the name of Christ's secret wife – and the V shape between the alleged couple, which some maintain is a reference to implicit femininity and fertility. Finally, the red and white clothes worn by Jesus and his feminized neighbour are mirror images of each other, which theorists take as a sign of their marriage. All of this is hard to accept on good faith alone, but almost impossible to dismiss out of hand.

Hook, Line and Sinker: the Priory of Sion Hoax

Many of the alleged 'facts' in *The Da Vinci Code* can be traced back not to the life of Christ, but rather to an elaborate 20th century hoax that began in the French town of Annemasse, and which for a while appeared to have the whole world fooled.

Its fleeting success was almost entirely thanks to the over-enthusiastic investigations of three men: Michael Baigent, Richard Leigh and Henry Lincoln. In their book *The Holy Blood And The Holy Grail*, the team claimed to have discovered evidence of a secret society based in a remote region of southern France – a society established following discoveries made in Jerusalem during the First Crusade in 1099, and sworn to protect the secret of the bloodline of Christ.

In reality, the Priory of Sion, as it was called, was actually formed on 20 July 1956 – and there are records in the local statute office to prove it. The hoax was the brainchild of a man

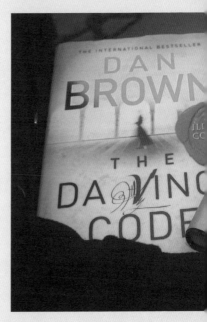

The authors of The Holy Blood And The Holy Grail *may have failed in their plagiarism lawsuit against Dan Brown's* The Da Vinci Code, *but the conspiracies at the heart of both books continue to capture the public imagination.*

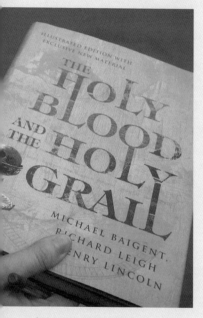

To this end, Plantard had a close friend forge various ancient manuscripts, which he then pretended had been discovered by one Father Francois Bérenger Saunière in a hollow pillar of his local church (dedicated, appropriately enough, to Mary Magdalene). Saunière's disproportionate wealth was then rumoured to have been the result of bribes offered by the Catholic Church in exchange for his continued silence about the discovery of the sect – in fact, he had made his fortune from collecting illegal payments for thousands of masses that he'd never even performed.

Either way, Baigent, Leigh and Lincoln were so excited at their discovery that they bought into it hook, line and sinker. Resulting revelations concerning the hoax didn't stop Dan Brown from incorporating the Priory of Sion as a central part of *The Da Vinci Code*, nor did they diminish sales of *The Holy Blood And The Holy Grail*, which is currently more popular than ever before.

named Pierre Plantard, who hoped that the people of France would be so convinced by his story that they would eventually also accept his fabricated claim of lineage to an ancient race of royals, and then seat him at his 'rightful' throne.

APPENDIX
Timeline of Vatican Events

30-64 AD

A fisherman by trade, Simon of Galilee becomes the closest of the Twelve Apostles to Jesus, who gives him the name Peter (from the Greek petra, meaning 'rock') when he says: "You are Peter, and on this rock I will build my church." (The discovery in 1968 of what are widely believed to be the Apostle's remains beneath St Peter's Basilica in the Vatican shows just how accurate a prediction this was.) Following the Ascension, Peter becomes the first Bishop of Rome, and thereby the first pope, until his execution by Nero (see below).

St Peter was both the first pope and the 'rock' upon which Christ founded his Church.

64 AD

Following the great fire of Rome, Emperor Nero persecutes the illegal cult of Christianity with unthinkable brutality – many live Christians are covered in wax and set on fire to illuminate Nero's garden parties; others he feeds indiscriminately to lions in the gladiatorial arena. Peter, meanwhile, is martyred by being crucified upside down on the site of what will later become St Peter's Basilica in the Vatican.

217-222 AD

Born into a life of slavery, Callistus is forced to flee after embezzling a large sum of his master's money. Captured trying to board a ship in Portus, he is returned to his master in the hope that he will recover some of the debt, but is soon rearrested for fighting with Jews in a local synagogue, after which he is condemned to the infamous mines of Sardinia. He is released through the intervention of the emperor's mistress and taken under the wing of Pope Victor I, whose place he eventually takes. Some

believe he was martyred by being thrown down a well.

296-304 AD

A shameless hypocrite, Marcellinus avoids persecution as a Christian by handing over holy scriptures to the Roman authorities and burning incense to pagan gods.

306 AD

Constantine becomes Roman Emperor. His mother, Helena, is a powerful Christian.

312 AD

While readying himself for the Battle of Milvian Bridge, Constantine gazes into the October sun and sees a vision of the cross and the first two letters of Christ's name, which he has emblazoned on his soldiers' shields. The battle is a resounding victory, which results in attitudes towards Christianity changing almost overnight.

313 AD

Constantine's Edict of Milan formally allows Christians freedom to practise their religion openly.

326 AD

Constantine orders the construction of a giant church on the site where St Peter was martyred. Completed 30 years later, this becomes the original St Peter's Basilica.

330 AD

The centre of the Roman Empire is shifted to Constantinople (now Istanbul in Turkey), creating a power vacuum in Rome that the Bishop of Rome – also known by the Greek for father, pappas (later 'pope') – is quick to fill.

382 AD

The books of the Bible are organized into the Old and New Testaments at a council called by Pope Damasus I. Simultaneously, Latin replaces Greek as the official language of Rome – it remains the official language of the Vatican to this day.

Constantine's Edict of Milan legitimized the previously illegal cult of Christianity, changing the fortunes of its followers virtually overnight.

Pope Leo I proves his diplomatic prowess by dissuading Attila the Hun from invading Rome in 452 AD – a shrewd move in the face of such a formidable enemy.

440-461 AD

A sound diplomat, in 452 Pope Leo I manages to persuade Attila the Hun not to invade Rome. He is unable to hold off an invasion by Gaeseric the Vandal three years later, but minimizes the damage by effectively ransoming the city. He is the first pope buried in St Peter's Basilica.

597 AD

While an abbot, Pope Gregory the Great is horrified at the sight of Anglo-Saxon slaves in Rome: "Not Angles," he says, "but angels." When elected pope, he sends St Augustine to England, where he converts King Ethelbert and the Anglo-Saxons from Celtic to Roman Christianity.

604-606 AD

Under Sabinian, the church sells grain to the poor in a time of great famine, a practice that makes him so unpopular that the people of Rome blockade the streets after his death and halt his funeral procession.

638 AD

Jerusalem (the place of Christ's birth, death and resurrection) is overrun by Muslim Saracens led by Caliph Omar.

649-653 AD

Martin I aggravates tensions between the papacy and the Roman Empire by refusing to seek Emperor Constans' approval following his election. Enraged, Constans has Martin dragged from his bed and ferried to Constantinople, where he is publicly flogged and sentenced to death – a decree later softened to exile in the Crimea. The church ignores his plight, and he dies five months after his arrival from cold and maltreatment at the hands of his captors.

795-816 AD

The Roman authorities take an instant dislike to Leo III, accusing him of perjury, adultery and selling papal indulgences. He is dragged into the street, beaten and threatened with having his tongue cut out, before being locked up in a monastery. He escapes and seeks refuge with the Frankish King Charlemagne, who returns him to Rome and reinstalls him as pope. On Christmas Day 800, Leo rewards Charlemagne by crowning him head of the new Holy Roman Empire, an institution that will remain in power until Napoleon invades and dissolves it more than 1,000 years later.

855 AD

Legend has it that a woman named Pope Joan reigns for three years before her femininity is uncovered on a procession through Rome (some say she actually gives birth unexpectedly). To this day, papal processions avoid the spot, where a memorial is maintained by believers.

963-964 AD

Few popes court controversy like John XII, who gambles openly, worships pagan gods and has those who oppose him blinded, castrated or murdered. He also turns the holy palace into a veritable whorehouse. John dies either at the hands of a jealous husband who catches him in flagrante with his wife, or of a stroke during the act itself.

984-985 AD

Pope Boniface VII locks the previous pope, John XIV, in the Castel Sant'Angelo and lets him starve to death. Such behaviour causes outrage: he is swiftly murdered, after which his naked corpse is dragged through the streets and mutilated by indignant Roman citizens.

Pope Boniface is arrested for his barbaric treatment of his predecessor.

1009

The Fatimid Caliph Al Hakim bi Amr Allah sacks the pilgrimage hospice in Jerusalem and partially destroys the Church of the Holy Sepulchre, built on the site of Christ's crucifixion and interment. Christians the world over are horrified.

1095

Pope Urban II offers assurances that anyone taking part in a holy war against the Muslims will automatically be pardoned for his sins and ensure his place in Heaven. Tens of thousands sign up, and the First Crusade begins in bloody earnest.

1099

The Crusaders retake Jerusalem with horrifying brutality but the Crusade is seen as a resounding success, although less than a century later the Holy Land is recaptured by the Arab Saladin, leading to no fewer than eight subsequent crusades that are anything but successful.

(1154-1159)

Educated at the still-running St Albans School before relocating to Rome via an Augustine monastery in France, Hadrian IV – real name Nicholas Breakspear – is the only Englishman ever to become Pope.

1198-1216

With the impotence of the Crusades painfully exposed, Innocent III decides to shift the papacy's religious zeal on to its own people, targeting the heretical Cathar community of southern France. In 1215, Innocent summons the Fourth Lateran Council, which requires Muslims and Jews to wear badges distinguishing them from Christians.

1232

The Inquisition is founded by Pope Gregory IX.

1276-1277

Soon after his election, John XXI has a private wing built for himself in the papal palace at Viterbo. His short reign as pope comes to an end swiftly after, when the ceiling of that same wing comes crashing down on him while he is sleeping.

1305

Clement V is elected pope amid such turmoil and waning papal authority that the entire papacy is relocated to Avignon in France at the invitation of King Philip VI.

Aware that the crusades were failing abroad, Pope Innocent III turned the wrath of the Church on its own kind.

1342-1352

Pope Clement VI transforms the Avignon papacy with his love of luxury, buying the city from the Queen of Naples for 80,000 gold florins, embellishing the papal palace with fine art and ensuring that musicians are constantly on hand to lift his spirits with song. Clement is not entirely materialistic, however, shunning the advice of his aides and administering close pastoral care to those unfortunates suffering from the Black Death, the first outbreak of which coincided with his reign,

Clement VI transformed the temporary Palace of the Popes in Avignon.

without ever contracting the disease himself. He leaves the papal coffers severely depleted when he dies.

1378

Pope Gregory XI moves an embattled papacy back to Rome. He dies later that year from stress-related illness.

1378-1389

Paranoid to the point of lunacy, Urban VI has six of his own cardinals imprisoned and tortured after convincing himself they are involved in a plot. He dies after falling from a mule; many suspect foul play.

1453

Constantinople falls to marauding Turks: like the Black Death that preceded it, this episode is believed by many to be divine retribution for the increasing indulgence and corruption of the papacy.

1478

Pope Sixtus IV authorizes the establishment of the Spanish Inquisition. During its 354-year reign, the Spanish Inquisition will sentence around 150,000

people for heresy, of whom roughly 5,000 will be executed.

1492-1503

As Alexander VI, Rodrigo Borgia rules by sheer terror and leaves behind a reputation like no other in papal history. His lusts turn Rome into a carnival of corruption, with prostitutes swarming the papal courts and murder going unpunished on an almost daily basis. His death, from poisoning, is not mourned: only when forced to do so will the priests at St Peter's Basilica accept his body for burial.

1503-1513

A born warrior, Julius II dons armour almost immediately after his election and leads his troops into battle, driving the despotic Cesare Borgia (son of Alexander VI) out of Italy and reclaiming great stretches of papal lands lost under previous popes. Julius is also a dedicated patron of the arts, commissioning many great works including Michelangelo's Sistine Chapel ceiling. In 1506, after having the original St Peter's Basilica torn down, Julius lays a foundation stone of the new basilica, and construction begins on the behemoth that dominates the Vatican today.

*Julius II was both a born warrior
and a patron of the arts.*

1517

Following a visit to Rome seven years previously, an appalled German priest named Martin Luther nails his *Ninety-Five Theses* – a scathing attack on papal corruption – to the door of a church in Wittenberg, setting in motion the Reformation and paving the path towards Protestantism.

Martin Luther burns a formal papal charter at the gates of Wittenberg in Germany.

1534

Henry VIII appeals to the pope on several occasions to grant the annulment of his marriage to Catherine of Aragon so that he can marry Anne Boleyn. The pope refuses. In a characteristic rage, Henry severs ties with Rome by passing the Act of Supremacy, which sets him up in place of the pope as head of the Church of England – another strike for the Reformation.

1540

Ignatius Loyola founds the Jesuit order as a force for spreading the pope's word abroad at a time of decimated papal authority. So begins the Catholic 'Counter-Reformation'.

1552

The Treaty of Passau recognises the legal right to practise Protestantism. European Christianity is split down the middle.

1557

The Vatican publishes an index of prohibited books, most of which remain under lock and key in the Vatican Secret Archives.

1623-1644

More than a century after work began, Urban VIII consecrates the newly completed St Peter's Basilica. He also cultivates relationships with contemporary artists and architects, including Gian Lorenzo Bernini, commissioning much of the interior

decoration and ensuring the proliferation of bees – the symbol of the pope's Barberini family – throughout the Vatican.

1633

Galileo Galilei is ordered to appear before the Inquisition for a second time to recant his hypothesis that the earth revolves around the sun – a flagrant challenge to the papacy's claim that the earth is at the centre of the universe. He finally recants under threat of torture and spends the rest of his life under house arrest.

1769-1774

Although a staunch supporter of the Jesuits, Clement XIV becomes pope at a time when the Catholic heads of Europe are demanding the dissolution of the order due to its perceived interference in their colonization of the Americas (Jesuit missionaries are the only ones standing up for the rights of native Americans). After deliberating for three years, Clement finally dissolves the Jesuits in 1773, significantly weakening the papacy and paving the way for the ultimate pillage of the indigenous American people. Guilt over his betrayal haunts him for the final months of his reign.

1793

The noble causes of the French Revolution are clouded by the 'Reign of Terror' that follows the establishment of the new French Republic, with Catholicism outlawed and many clergymen among the 20,000 people executed for the cause.

1798

Pope Pius VI struggles to maintain amiable relations with the post-revolutionary French government, and finds himself powerless when Napoleon's troops enter the gates of Rome, forcing Pius into exile and declaring a new Roman Republic. When he dies the following year, many believe it marks the end of the papacy.

1806

Napoleon dissolves the Holy Roman Empire more than 1,000 years after its creation.

Pope Clement XIV's decision to dissolve the Jesuits haunted him until the day he died.

Pius VII travelled all the way to Fontainebleau (pictured here) to meet the young Napoleon, but left snubbed and humiliated, and their relationship soon turned sour.

1800-1823

Pius VII attempts to regain papal prestige by travelling to Paris in 1804 to officially crown Napoleon, but is snubbed by the young Emperor and forced to leave in humiliation. Napoleon eventually seizes the Papal States and has Pius arrested and sent into captivity, where he remains until Napoleon's defeat in 1814.

1831-1846

Conservative to the point of caricature, Gregory XVI goes so far as to ban the use of railways in the Papal States, calling them 'ways of the devil'.

1846-1878

When revolutionary forces assassinate the Prime Minister of the Papal States and seize Rome in 1848, Pius IX flees to central Italy before being returned to Rome by French troops. In an attempt to consolidate waning papal power, he convenes the First Vatican Council (1869), which establishes the notion of 'papal infallibility' – ie, that it is literally impossible for the pope to err in

his judgements. When the French troops are withdrawn in 1870, Pius declares himself "a prisoner in the Vatican".

1922-1939

An enthusiastic mountaineer and the first pope to grace the airwaves of Vatican Radio, Pius views communism as a greater threat to the world than Hitler's National Socialism, signing a concordat with Germany in 1933 on the advice of the then papal ambassador to Germany, Eugene Pacelli (soon to be Pope Pius XII). Later, horrified at Nazi atrocities, he pens a speech denouncing the forces of fascism worldwide; he dies hours before he is due to give it, and the text of the speech miraculously disappears. Rumours that he has been murdered by pro-fascist forces within the Vatican (even the father of Mussolini's mistress) are very quick to circulate.

1939-1958

Pius XII's relationship with Mother Pasqualina, his devout German housekeeper, is the cause of much cynicism and more than a few sordid rumours, although it is his relationship with Nazi Germany that does the most damage to his legacy. On good terms with Hitler since his days as papal ambassador to Germany, Pius does little to stem the increasing aggression of the Nazis, fails to speak out against the Holocaust and finally allows SS guards to round up Roman Jews from under his nose. His death is blighted by a botched embalming that accelerates the rotting of his corpse and embarrasses the Vatican for years to come.

1968

The Vatican announces that bones discovered beneath the high altar of St Peter's Basilica are indeed the remains of the Apostle Peter himself.

1929

The Lateran Treaty creates the Vatican State – the smallest independent nation on earth – and guarantees independent sovereignty for the Holy See.

1978

Forgoing the elaborate ceremonial coronation (he is instead inaugurated at a solemn outdoor mass), Pope John Paul I dies after just 33 days in office. Rumours of an untimely assassination once again pervade the Vatican.

1978-2005

Once an enthusiastic poet, playwright and actor, it is nevertheless in his popular role as the 'Outdoor Pope' that the athletic John Paul II infuriates traditionalists, never more so than when he has a swimming pool built in the papal summer residence, where paparazzi later snap him in his trunks. In 1981, he barely survives an assassination attempt in St Peter's Square, going on to work for over two more decades before finally succumbing to a lingering illness in 2005. His passing is much mourned across the world.

2005

Cardinal Joseph Ratzinger's election to the papacy as Benedict XVI causes a huge stir among insiders afraid he will usher in an age of renewed Catholic conservatism. Their fears are founded on the new pope's early days as Prefect of the Congregation for the Doctrine of the Faith (formerly an offshoot of the Papal Inquisition), during which he provided a hardline 'bad cop' to the affable face of the papacy as presented by John Paul II, preaching against homosexuality, birth control and various liberal movements, even penning a controversial letter condemning feminism for making 'homosexuality and heterosexuality virtually equivalent'.

The early days of his papacy, however, confound his critics: Benedict appears far more genial and personable than predicted, even taking to riding around in an open-topped popemobile in an effort to become closer to the people. His edicts seem similarly open-minded – at the time of going to press, he was even believed to be considering easing the papal ban on contraception – but there are hints of an underlying conservatism, as seen in a recently leaked letter, dating from 2001, which forbids all members of the Catholic Church from speaking publicly about the paedophile priest scandal on pain of excommunication. A former member of the Hitler Youth, Benedict also causes controversy in May 2006 by visiting the former concentration camp at Auschwitz and making what many Jews see as an insulting speech.

*Pope Benedict XVI (2005 –) has embraced his new role with open arms,
but controversy has never been far behind him.*

Sources

Part One

Allen, John L. – *All The Pope's Men: The Inside Story Of How The Vatican Really Thinks* (Doubleday Books, 2004)

Castle, Tony and McGrath, Peter – *On This Rock, The Popes And Their Times: St Peter to John Paul II* (St Paul's Publishing, 2002)

Wilson, A. N. – *Jesus* (Flamingo, 1992)

Part Two

Bello, Nino Lo – *The Incredible Book Of Vatican Facts And Papal Curiosities* (Liguori Publications, 1998)

Hanley, Anne (Ed) – *Time Out Guides: Rome* (Time Out Guides Ltd, 2005)

Part Three

Hoffman, Paul – *Anatomy Of The Vatican: An Irreverent View Of The Holy See* (Robert Hale, 1984)

McDowell, Bart – *Inside The Vatican* (National Geographic Books, 2005)

Reese, Thomas J. – *Inside The Vatican: The Politics And Organization Of The Catholic Church* (Harvard University Press, 1998)

Part Four

Cornwell, John – *A Thief In The Night: Life And Death In The Vatican* (Penguin, 2001)

Cornwell, Rupert – *God's Banker: The Life And Death Of Roberto Calvi* (Harper Collins, 1984)

Follain, John – *City Of Secrets: The Startling Truth Behind The Vatican Murders* (Harper Paperbacks, 2003)

Williams, Paul L. – *The Vatican Exposed: Money, Murder And The Mafia* (Prometheus Books, 2003)

Yallop, David – *In God's Name* (Jonathan Cape, 1984)

Part Five

Allen, John L – *Opus Dei: Secrets And Power Inside The Catholic Church* (Allen Lane, 2005)

Ambrosini, Luisa – *Secret Archives Of The Vatican* (Eyre & Spottiswoode, 1970)

Baigent, Michael, Leigh, Richard and Lincoln, Henry – *The Holy Blood And The Holy Grail* (Arrow, 1996)

Cornwell, John – *Hitler's Pope: The Secret History Of Pius XII* (Penguin, 2003)

Escriva, Josemaria – *The Way: The Essential Classic Of Opus Dei's Founder* (Image, 2006)

Picture credits